Bolly wood Super stars

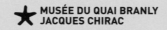

Bolly wood Super stars

A Short Story of Indian Cinema

Edited by
Julien Rousseau and Hélène Kessous

This catalogue was published on the occasion of the *Bollywood Superstars: A Short Story of Indian Cinema* exhibition, organised by Louvre Abu Dhabi, Musée du Quai Branly – Jacques Chirac, and France Muséums, and held at Louvre Abu Dhabi from 25 January to 4 June 2023 and at Musée du Quai Branly – Jacques Chirac from 26 September 2023 to 7 January 2024.

Sponsored by

PUREHEALTH+

Exhibition Season Partner

Curatorship

Julien Rousseau
Curator, Head of the Asian Collections, Musée du Quai Branly – Jacques Chirac

Hélène Kessous
PhD in Social Anthropology and Ethnology, École des Hautes Études en Sciences Sociales

Organisation

Department of Culture and Tourism – Abu Dhabi

H.E. Mohamed Khalifa Al Mubarak
Chairman

H.E. Saood Abdulaziz Al Hosani
Undersecretary

H.E. Saeed Al Fazari
Executive Director, Strategic Affairs

H.E. Saleh Mohamed Al Geziry
General Director, Tourism

Adnan Al Awadhi
Executive Director, Support Services Sector

Rita Aoun-Abdo
Executive Director, Culture Sector

Mohammad Al Frehat
General Counsel

Louvre Abu Dhabi

Manuel Rabaté
Director

Marwa Rubayee Al Menhali
Director, Support Services

Souraya Noujaim
Director, Scientific, Curatorial and Collection Management

Lamya Al Nuaimi
Director, Development, Marketing and Communications

Ahmed Al Balooshi
Acting Director, Technical Operations

Ugo Bertoni
Acting Director, External Affairs, Outreach and Cultural Engagement

Kyron Portwig
Acting Director, Visitor Experience and Sales

Nawar Omar Belshalat
Manager, Strategy

Tariq Saleh Al Ameri
Manager, Procurement and Contracts

Sana Ibrahim Al Hammadi
Manager, Digital Marketing

Majed Al Hashly
Manager, Communications

Mohamed Jama Al Musharakh
Manager, Marketing

Mohammed Naji Alnuaimi
Manager, Finance

Alia Saeed Alshamsi
Manager, Cultural Programming

Maral Jule Bedoyan
Manager, Education and Learning Resources

Michelle Carswell
Human Resources Advisor

Laura Coll
Manager, Visitor Operations

Theofanis Karafotias
Manager, Museography & Collection Management

Amine Kharchach
Manager, Interpretation and Mediation

Fargia Lamrabet
Manager, Information Technology

Amanda Nicole Smith
Head, Publications Section

Ruby Wiltshire
Manager, Events

Exhibition

Souraya Noujaim
Director, Scientific, Curatorial and Collection Management

Alice Querin
Acting Temporary Exhibition Unit Head

Jeanne Rethacker
Senior Curatorial Assistant

Aisha AlAhmadi
Curatorial Assistant

Publications

Ugo Bertoni
Acting Director, External Affairs, Outreach and Cultural Engagement

Amanda Nicole Smith
Head, Publications Section

Mohamed Zaggar
Senior Editor

Brian Kerrigan
Senior Visual and Images Officer

Hessa Alkhyeli
Senior Production Officer

Noora Suhail Alameri
Image Database Associate

Louvre Abu Dhabi would like to thank all teams across the various departments for their invaluable contribution to this exhibition.

France Muséums

Hervé Barbaret
Chief Executive Officer

Sandra Lagumina
President of the Board of Directors

Laurence des Cars
President of the Scientific Council

Stéphane-Arnaud Roisin
Deputy CEO

Anne Eschapasse
Managing Director – Abu Dhabi

Samuel Taïeb
General Secretary

Adrien Berthelot
Director of Loans and Acquisitions

Jean-Michel Carré
Director of Consulting and Research

Olivia Davidson
Director of Exhibitions and Publications

Luc Piralla
Scientific Director

Julie d'Enfert
Project Development Manager

Zélie Roche
Institutional Affairs and CSR Manager

Exhibition and Publications

Olivia Davidson
Director of Exhibitions and Publications

Francesca Crudo
Project Manager

Pauline Vernières
Temporary Exhibitions Officer

Sandra Mazière
Deputy to Director of Exhibitions
and Publications, Chief Registrar

Chloé Guillaume
Registrar

Sabrina Mathieu
Senior Museography Project Manager

Mihai Cristian Voicu
Museography Operations
Project Manager

Mathilde Etot
Interpretation and Education Manager

Orlane Lefeuvre
Interpretation
and Programming Officer

Tiphaine Gourlay
In-House Legal Counsel

Sébastien Cotte
Digital Manager

Céline Moulard
Freelance Editor for France Muséums

Amélie Despérier
Freelance Editorial Coordinator
for France Muséums

Musée du Quai Branly – Jacques Chirac

Emmanuel Kasarhérou
President

Jérôme Bastianelli
Deputy Managing Director

Angélique Delorme
Associate Deputy
Managing Director

Anne-Solène Rolland
Director of Heritage
and Collections

Philippe Charlier
Director of Research
and Education

Christine Drouin
Director of Cultural Development

Christophine Erignac
Director of Sponsorship

Céline Féraudy
Director of Administration
and Human Resources

David Jolly
Director of Management Control

Benoit Martin
Director of Technical
Resources and Security

Isabelle Rouls
Director of Public and Education

Myriam Simonneaux
Director of Communication

Yves Touboulic
Director of Accounting

Exhibitions Department

Isabelle Lainé
Head of the Exhibitions Department

Marie Ormevil
Exhibition Officer,
Deputy to the Head
of Exhibitions Department

Sylvia Linard
Registrar, Deputy to the Head
of Exhibitions Department

Quiterie d'Aries
Registrar

Domitille Chaudieu
Exhibition Officer

Touring Exhibitions and International Development Department

Fred Chih-Chia Chung
Head of Department,
Deputy Director
of Cultural Development

Safia Belmenouar
Touring Exhibitions Coordinator

Exhibition

Scenography
Atelier Maciej Fiszer:
Maciej Fiszer, Marion Forissier

Graphics
CL Design:
Nicolas Journé, Nicolas Pellerin

Audio-visual and Multimedia Interpretation
Artistic Creative Company:
Arno Creignou, Pierre Guillaud-Lux,
Alex Waltz, Hugo Scialom,
Matthieu Dallaporta

Audio-visual and Multimedia engineering
Approche Audiovisuel:
Laurent Oberlé

Lighting
Hi lighting Design Production:
Benoit Deseille

Structural Engineering Consultant
Bollinger+Grohmann:
Julien Delayre, Narjis Lemrini

Iconography
Le Chaînon Manquant:
Catherine Paoli, Agnès Bellec,
Jessica Darmon, Ava Balzano,
Cécile Clarens

Acknowledgments

The quality of this exhibition is due to the generosity of the public and private institutions, as well as the collectors, who have loaned exceptional works. We would like to express our sincere gratitude to them:

Louvre Abu Dhabi, United Arab Emirates
Manuel Rabaté
Director

Souraya Noujaim
Director, Scientific, Curatorial and Collection Management

Musée du Quai Branly – Jacques Chirac, France
Emmanuel Kasarhérou
President

Musée de l'Armée, France
General Henry de Medlege
Director

Musée National des Arts Asiatiques – Guimet, France
Sophie Makariou
President

Al-Sabah Collection, Dar al-Athar al-Islamiyah, Kuwait
Sheikha Hussa Sabah
al-Salem al-Sabah
Director General

Priya Paul Collection, India

Raja Ravi Varma Heritage Foundation, India
Gitanjali Maini
Managing Trustee and CEO

The Musée du Quai Branly – Jacques Chirac would also like to thank the additional lenders for the Paris exhibition:

Bibliothèque Nationale de France, France
Laurence Engel
President

Cinémathèque Française, France
Costa-Gavras
President

Victoria and Albert Museum, United Kingdom
Tristram Hunt
Director

For their trust and valuable assistance, the curators and organisers of the exhibition would like to thank:
Nick Barnard, Adrien Bossard, Laurence Briot, Katia Cartacheff, Pauline Chougnet, Véronique Declercq, Virginia Fienga, Hélène Gascuel, Sundari Gobalakichenane, Laurent Héricher, Anna Jackson, Amin Jaffer, Caroline Laurent, Vincent Lefèvre, Delon Madavan, Amina Okada, Agilan Pajaniradja, Laure Parchomenko, Divia Patel, François Picard, Marine Pichard, Sylvie Pimpaneau, Luc Piralla, Anne-Solène Rolland, Catherine Servan-Schreiber.

Special thanks to Film Heritage Foundation.

Catalogue Authors

Amandine D'Azevedo
Associate Professor,
Film and Audiovisual Studies,
University Paul Valéry
– Montpellier 3

Swarnavel Eswaran
Associate Professor,
Department of English
and the School of Journalism,
Michigan State University

Hélène Kessous
PhD in Social Anthropology
and Ethnology, École des Hautes
Études en Sciences Sociales

Eva Markovits
Programmer and Selector,
Film critic for *Cahiers du cinéma*

Jeanne Rethacker
Senior Curatorial Assistant,
Louvre Abu Dhabi

Julien Rousseau
Curator, Head of the Asian
Collections, Musée du Quai Branly
– Jacques Chirac

Némésis Srour
PhD in Social Anthropology
and Ethnology

Selvaraj Velayutham
Associate Professor, Macquarie
School of Social Sciences

Ophélie Wiel
Author and Specialist in Indian
Cinema, Lecturer in the History
of Silent and Classical Cinema,
University of Paris 3
– Sorbonne Nouvelle

CONTENTS

Illustrations followed by an asterisk (*) indicate works presented only at the exhibition of the Musée du Quai Branly – Jacques Chirac

Foreword

Mohamed Khalifa Al Mubarak
Chairman, Department
of Culture and Tourism – Abu Dhabi

Bollywood Superstars: A Short Story of Indian Cinema takes us on an awe-inspiring journey through time as we explore India's centuries-old storytelling traditions, from early folklore to the glamour of today's big screen. This remarkable collection encapsulates the colour, passion, and diversity that the subcontinent has bestowed on the Gulf region via the arts.

It reminds us, too, of the deep cultural ties and social connections that the United Arab Emirates shares with our close friends and neighbours across the Arabian Sea. Our country has long held a special bond with India, reaching back to when merchants from the Indus Valley, capturing the trade winds of the monsoon, first sailed to the Arabian Peninsula around 3000 BCE to trade timber, spices, and grain in return for copper, pottery, and more. Beyond our crucial economic ties, vibrant cultural exchange between India and the United Arab Emirates continues to flourish.

In June 2022, Abu Dhabi proudly hosted the prestigious International Indian Film Academy Awards ceremony for the first time, welcoming to our shores the stars and masterminds of the industry, including Bollywood celebrity couple Abhishek Bachchan and Aishwarya Rai Bachchan and the brilliant Composer A. R. Rahman. And in two years' time, Abu Dhabi will complete the nation's first traditional Hindu temple in the capital's Abu Mureikha district, reflecting the United Arab Emirates' ongoing mission to build a nation of peace and tolerance.

Now, *Bollywood Superstars* aims to both surprise and delight visitors by capturing the essence of India's magical cinematic culture, whose artists, stories, and themes are intensely popular and resonate so strongly within our own society.

The fact that the exhibition is taking place at Louvre Abu Dhabi complements the ongoing efforts to position Abu Dhabi as a hub for the regional film industry. Under the umbrella of the Creative Media Authority, entities such as Abu Dhabi Film Commission, Image Nation Abu Dhabi, and Arab Film Studio continue to showcase stories that are relevant both locally and internationally while promoting Abu Dhabi as an ideal location for production and post-production.

It has been said that cinema is a universal language, with the power to transcend cultures and borders. It is my hope that everyone who experiences the *Bollywood Superstars* exhibition, Abu Dhabi residents and visitors alike, will come away with both a deeper understanding and greater respect for India's achievements and influence in this much-loved art form.

Foreword

Hervé Barbaret
Chief Executive Officer, France Muséums

Sandra Lagumina
President, Board of Directors,
France Muséums

From its very beginning, Louvre Abu Dhabi was envisioned as a bridge between cultures and eras, an invitation to discover 'the other'. Each of the museum's exhibitions aims to renew our vision of the world.

This time, Louvre Abu Dhabi shines a spotlight on a paradoxical scenario: while Indian cinema produces the largest number of films internationally, seen by hundreds of millions of viewers each year, it remains largely unknown in some parts of the world. Although the exhibition is entitled *Bollywood Superstars: A Short Story of Indian Cinema*, it does not limit itself to the specificity of the cinema produced in Bombay (present-day Mumbai), known as Bollywood, nor to its famous star system. On the contrary, it invites us to explore an abundant and multi-faceted art, just like the country from which it originates. This art form combines the various influences of an extremely rich and centuries-old visual culture: theatre, painting, dance, song, sculpture, and more. This abundance results in a tremendous variety of cinema in India, which ranges from hugely popular films with actors that border on the demigod-level, such as Shah Rukh Khan, to Satyajit Ray's challenging works. The exhibition sets out to discover how the vibrant and diverse types of Indian cinema have created a specific culture and imagery, which contributes to the unity of the country-subcontinent and to its international influence.

Proof of the success of previous collaborations, the *Bollywood Superstars* exhibition is the outcome of a new partnership with the Musée du Quai Branly – Jacques Chirac. It also benefits from many exceptional loans from international collections and major French partner museums, such as the Musée de l'Armée and the Musée National des Arts Asiatiques – Guimet. This exhibition has also given us the opportunity to forge new ties with non-Western institutions, particularly the Indian Film Institute and the Raja Ravi Varma Heritage Foundation.

For a museum, making the moving image the central subject of an exhibition involves many challenges, which have resulted in a dialogue between the films and artwork. We would like to acknowledge the outstanding work that has been done in the area of interpretive content. New devices have been imagined, inspired by the first objects used to project moving images. Magic lanterns and bioscopes have underpinned the concept for a wide variety of objects, highlighting the interconnectivity of cinema with other art forms.

We would like to thank our partners and collaborators, the exhibition curators Julien Rousseau, Head of the Asian Collections at the Musée du Quai Branly – Jacques Chirac, and Hélène Kessous, a specialist in Indian cinema with a PhD in social anthropology and ethnology. We would also like to acknowledge the work of the France Muséums and Louvre Abu Dhabi teams for their unwavering commitment.

How can we pay homage to the richness of Indian cinema, which tells stories and astounds its audience, better than by giving in to the temptation to create a narrative? Hence, the exhibition outlines the contours of this spectacular world, a world in which visitors are invited to explore, adding a new chapter to the grand history of Louvre Abu Dhabi.

Foreword

Manuel Rabaté
Director, Louvre Abu Dhabi

We are proud to welcome *Bollywood Superstars: A Short Story of Indian Cinema* to Louvre Abu Dhabi. This exhibition comes to the museum as it celebrates its fifth anniversary and demonstrates yet again our enduring commitment to showcase the wealth of cultures that define so much of life in the United Arab Emirates.

Our staff and partners have worked tirelessly to bring together the most ambitious collection of artworks that are at the heart of Indian society and popular culture. We hope that by offering a tantalising glimpse into the subcontinent's rich and diverse filmmaking history, visitors can better understand the myriad of our shared roots, common values, and cultural connections.

I would like to take this opportunity to offer my profound thanks to all of our prestigious partners who have helped bring this remarkable exhibition to fruition. In particular, I would like to acknowledge our second collaboration with Musée du Quai Branly – Jacques Chirac, Paris, as well as the enormous generosity of Musée National des Arts Asiatiques – Guimet, Paris; Musée de l'Armée, Paris; al-Sabah Collection, Kuwait City; Priya Paul Collection, New Delhi; and the Raja Ravi Varma Heritage Foundation, Bengaluru. This exhibition would not have been possible without the work of France Muséums, who has been producing Louvre Abu Dhabi exhibitions since the museum's opening, and the dedication of the curatorial and collection teams at Louvre Abu Dhabi led by Souraya Noujaim, especially Aisha AlAhmadi and Jeanne Rethacker.

I would also like to thank the exhibition's co-curators: Julien Rousseau, Head of the Asian Collections at the Musée du Quai Branly – Jacques Chirac, and Anthropologist Hélène Kessous, who specialises in South Asian cinema, both of whom deserve infinite acclaim for their creativity and dedication.

Finally, I'd like to express my huge appreciation to all those involved in Abu Dhabi's thriving film industry, with particular thanks to the emirate's Creative Media Authority and the Abu Dhabi Film Commission. Today, India is the world's leading film producer, creating more than 1,500 films a year in around twenty languages exported throughout Asia, the Middle East, and Africa. Hindi classics have been playing in the United Arab Emirates' independent theatres since the 1960s, their popularity buoyed by geographical proximity, family values, and even linguistic similarities. More recently, Bollywood and its stars have become wildly popular in the Arab world by encapsulating the glamour, fashion, and epic storytelling that both cultures share.

Through the photographs, costumes, and film extracts, the exhibition intends to portray a sense of spectacle and escapism to all art lovers. Indian visitors, who represent such an important part of our audience at Louvre Abu Dhabi, can also make use of our Hindi multimedia guides.

Whether it be immersing yourself in our pre-cinema artefacts such as a travelling storyteller's portable wooden shrine, or stepping inside a breath-taking, reconstructed Indian cinema, this exhibition exemplifies the museum's mission to open minds and stimulate dialogue in fun and imaginative ways.

Indian cinema is vast and multicultural, as well as being packed with stories that resonate with our own lives. I believe that celebrating these commonalities through art and creativity gives us an enormous sense of joy. I hope you do, too.

Foreword

President, Musée du Quai Branly
– Jacques Chirac

The exhibition *Bollywood Superstars: A Short Story of Indian Cinema* explores the affinity that binds India to cinema. Visitors will discover why this medium, which was introduced in 1896, acted as a developing bath for the country's identity, at times reinforcing its diversity and embracing its many facets, while at other times contributing to the building of a strong pan-Indian consciousness, especially in response to the British colonial occupation.

The dissemination of cinema across the subcontinent coincided with India's rich tradition of narrative folk arts (travelling storytellers' paintings, shadow theatre, magic lanterns). This tradition moved the gods out of the temples and brought them closer to their worshippers. These practices that created visualisations of the revered gods would eventually grow into the virtual deification of film stars. The audience will also grasp the extent that Bollywood's emblematic music and choreography are derived from the Indian propensity to combine the arts – dance, theatre, sculpture, painting...

An exhibition of visual anthropology, *Bollywood Superstars* explores the multiple aesthetics of Indian cinema, revealing a variety of narrative and stylistic repertoires that mirror the diversity of the country's histories, local identities, and languages. It should also be noted that Bollywood is one of many regional industries, such as Tollywood, Mollywood, or Kollywood. The section dedicated to the realist Filmmaker Satyajit Ray illustrates the plurality of these narratives.

The curators of this exhibition are Julien Rousseau, Head of the Asian Collections at the Musée du Quai Branly – Jacques Chirac, and Anthropologist Hélène Kessous, specialising in India. I would like to acknowledge the thoroughness and clarity of their work, as Indian cinema can be approached from countless perspectives.

Extraordinary artworks are displayed alongside the film extracts screened in the exhibition. I would like to thank Louvre Abu Dhabi, Musée National des Arts Asiatiques – Guimet, Musée de l'Armée, al-Sabah Collection, Raja Ravi Varma Heritage Foundation and all the private collections for their generosity. Their loans complement the pieces from the Quai Branly collection.

Manuel Rabaté, Director of Louvre Abu Dhabi, is the initiator of this project. He played a decisive role in its execution, together with Souraya Noujaim, Scientific, Curatorial and Collection Management Director. I would like to thank them both for their trust. Thanks also to Olivia Davidson, Exhibitions and Publications Director at France Muséums, and to Francesca Crudo, Project Manager, who have both made essential contributions to the project.

The exhibition *Bollywood Superstars* stands out for the quality and originality of its content. Before being showcased at the Musée du Quai Branly – Jacques Chirac in September 2023, it is sure to appeal to visitors at Louvre Abu Dhabi, an institution whose vitality and influence we are honoured to be associated with.

Preface

Souraya Noujaim
Director, Scientific, Curatorial
and Collection Management,
Louvre Abu Dhabi

Louvre Abu Dhabi possesses key examples of Indian art in its collections, including a remarkable set of 'miniatures' – or more precisely, single illustrated album pages – collected by Filmmaker James Ivory.

Consisting of 99 works created between the 16th and late 19th centuries, this collection highlights several aspects of the incredibly rich and multifaceted tradition of Indian painting. Two sheets within this set exemplify the production of the imperial Mughal workshops, the most famous workshops to both specialists and the general public. However, James Ivory was also interested in other schools and styles, particularly in Rajput miniatures. This collection was obtained quite by chance by the filmmaker, around 1958, while he was still a film student. The discovery of the set in a San Francisco gallery led him to create a short film on Indian miniatures entitled *The Sword and the Flute* (1959), and then to travel to India, which played a major role in shaping his career and life.

Through their themes, colours, inventiveness, fantasy, and the way they combine various influences (Indian, European, Mughal, Rajput, Muslim and Hindu), these miniatures seem to anticipate today's popular and world-renowned Bollywood cinema, whose name comes from the contraction of Bombay and Hollywood.

Just like Indian cinema, whose origins are recounted through a display of objects, posters, photographs, film excerpts, and location reconstructions, including a shadow play and an authentic Indian cinema, miniatures illustrate mythological or religious stories, court scenes, scenes from daily life or rural life, and even romances. They also blend Eastern and Western influences. The contribution of photography and the moving image, and later commercial cinema, at the end of the 19th and the beginning of the 20th centuries was, of course, a major difference. Silent films, then talkies, favoured spectacular subjects, emotion, fictional stories, music, and dance, thereby allowing the most daring combinations. The permanent display of our museum's collection analyses this major role played by photography and film.

In keeping with the spirit of our collection and our approach, the exhibition *Bollywood Superstars: A Short Story of Indian Cinema*, reaches its full meaning. This exhibition, which is co-organised by Louvre Abu Dhabi, the Musée du Quai Branly – Jacques Chirac and France Muséums, features some 65 artworks and 44 film excerpts. Curated by Julien Rousseau, Head of the Asian Collections at the Musée du Quai Branly – Jacques Chirac, with Anthropologist Hélène Kessous as scientific advisor, the exhibition celebrates the power of the image and evokes the fascination exerted today by these films' iconic actors, celebrated as heroes in India.

Although it cannot on its own encapsulate the diversity of the Indian subcontinent's film production, Bollywood has become a highly popular transnational cultural phenomenon. With an annual production of around 1,500 films translated into twenty languages and distributed throughout Asia, the Middle East and Africa, India is indeed one of the leaders of the film industry today.

The exhibition is organised in three sequences with one focus. The first sequence outlines the various forms of creation and dissemination of popular culture before the birth of cinema. It covers a spectrum that embraces travelling storytellers, shadow plays, and magic lanterns – the forerunner of the moving image – as well as showcasing traditional regional dances. While their popularity is no longer the same, these art forms haven't disappeared with the rise of cinema, and often coexist with travelling film screenings, for instance, whose tradition persists in India, as evidenced by the special mention for L'Œil d'or Award in 2016 at the Cannes Film Festival to a similar itinerant initiative.

The second sequence begins with a presentation of the work of the renowned Painter and Illustrator Ravi Varma (1848–1906). The popular imagery produced in massive quantities in his workshops had a profound influence on the aesthetics of early Indian cinema. After studying with European painters at the court of Travancore, Varma became known for his portrayals of mythological scenes and stories from popular literature, which he recreated in a style that was both theatrical and naturalistic. He also developed techniques for producing affordable colour images. His representations of Hindu deities, which are found on the market today, played a significant role in popular devotion. The second part of this sequence is dedicated to the evolution from royal portraits to historical films.

In the second half of the 19th century, photography was a spectacular medium for staging power. Rulers adopted it and incorporated it into the codes of royal portraiture. Like miniatures, which are also striking and colourful images that provide detailed descriptions of the court's splendour, cinema adapts these conventions. The Mughal and Rajput dynasties are often used as backdrops for historical and sentimental films. A special focus on Satyajit Ray and his social cinema punctuates the visit.

This interlude is followed by the third sequence of the exhibition, dedicated to Bollywood superstars from the 1970s to 2020. In India, these actors who interpret charismatic characters are genuinely worshipped. The film genres often mirror those of popular international productions or television series, including melodramas, musicals, social and family films, thrillers, historical dramas and superhero films, among others, which are interspersed with regional songs and dances.

Particular efforts have been made to create a specific atmosphere for the scenography of the exhibition with strong theatrical qualities, taking elements of colours, ambience and lighting from the Indian films. In the first sequence, for example, a shadow play is reconstructed, with its typical characters such as the demon monkeys or the heroes. In the second sequence, a wall of images illustrates the Indian mythological imaginary, where visitors are immersed in the world of Hindu deities. The focus on Satyajit Ray's realistic work provides an opportunity to see the photos and storyboards of his films on the big screen. Finally, the last sequence of the exhibition features a faithful reconstruction of an authentic Indian cinema, accessed through a corridor covered with colourful posters and portraits of the most celebrated stars.

From Indian miniature art to the successful entertainment industry that Bollywood has become, a number of patterns can be identified. The cross-influences that arise in the former are found in the latter, multiplied tenfold by technological improvements. This underlines the continued presence of the great mythological and literary narratives in Indian culture, and the vitality of its regional cultures.

Satyavadi Harishchandra (1917), by Dadasaheb Phalke (see cat. 18, page 69)

History of Pre-cinema Devices and the Birth of Cinema

'To appeal to everyone within a national community which was still an abstract concept at the turn of the 20th century, the first films honoured gods and heroes that were then thought to be shared by the entire Indian subcontinent.'

The Gods of the Silver Screen: From Mythology to Star System

**JULIEN ROUSSEAU
AND HÉLÈNE KESSOUS**

A CINEMA WITH INDIAN ROOTS

In 1896, Marius Sestier, the Lumière brothers' cinematograph operator in India, presented the first screenings in the country, allowing a Bombay (present-day Mumbai) audience to witness the birth of cinema less than a year after the Parisians did.

From 1900 onwards, the number of players in the burgeoning world of cinematograph increased and within a few years; Indian and European distributors, projectionists, and operators began to travel across the country to show the newly available films. Bombay, Calcutta (present-day Kolkata) and Madras (Chennai) became the cradles of this flourishing industry. Its initial audience was not only the British living in India, but also the Indian elite, and those who shared similar interests. From the beginning, the players in this new economic market aspired to make Indian cinema a mass phenomenon, modelling itself off of the industry in the United States, that would be called Hollywood a few years later. However, beyond economic aspects, and beyond the establishment of the network and infrastructure necessary for the expansion of this new medium, the birth of Indian cinema also coincided with protests against the British Empire. As a vehicle for building national consciousness, cinema had to create an identity that was foremost 'Indian'.

1.
In *Bollywood Film Studio ou comment les films se font à Bombay*, Emmanuel Grimaud quotes a statement by Dadasaheb Phalke explaining that films have to be made for someone and are intended for a specific audience. He advocated for his regional vision of filmmaking by using the example of a film about Shivaji – a purely Marathi theme – which would not appeal to a Calcutta or Madras audience. Despite the mobility of populations in India today, and the fact that there may be enough Marathis in Calcutta to consider a release in Bengal of a film on Shivaji, cinema is now more regionally focused than ever.

2.
The directors of these first films were members of the Brahmin elite.

But how could a national and pan-Indian identity be achieved in a country ruled by the British Empire, divided by languages, castes, and religions, as well as being characterised by strong multiculturalism? At a very early stage, cinema faced these challenges, and still does today. With its complex linguistic situation, India is comprised of 28 states, 8 union territories and 24 official languages, but the country was even more diverse and fragmented at the time of the British Empire.

Could a film about Bengal be understood in Madras? Could it transcend regional divisions?[1]

To appeal to everyone within a national community which was still an abstract concept at the turn of the 20th century, the first films honoured gods and heroes that were then thought to be shared by the entire Indian subcontinent.[2] Cinema would return to the roots of Indian civilisation and pursue its artistic traditions while offering its own interpretation of texts, images, and costumes. Like the visual arts that predated it, cinema would create living religious images.

EMBODYING THE GODS

Whether through the sheer monumentality of medieval temples, the vibrant colours of Rajput miniatures, or the magic of the first moving images, the religious arts express the presence and universal influence of the gods by using the media of the time. Although cinema is not limited to mythological subjects, it belongs to a cultural and religious heritage which, over the centuries, has raised images to the status of living icons. From 800 to 400 BCE, following the Vedic period which had left a great void in the history of art, texts known generically as the Upanishads theorised important philosophical and religious concepts such as karma (the sum of actions) and samsara (the cycle of reincarnation), as well as the possibility of uniting the individual with the universal, summed up by the mantra of non-duality (*tat tvam asi*, which literally means 'that thou art'). The criticism of the ritualism and elitism of ancient Brahmanism paved the way for a devotional Hinduism (*bhakti*), in which worshippers can attain liberation through knowledge, devotion, and offerings (*puja*) mediated by images inhabited by the gods. Alongside the official public cults of worship, traditionally funded by the ruling warrior elite (*kshatriya*) and enforced by the priestly class (Brahmin), popular religion favoured a direct and internalised relationship with the gods, sometimes comparing the body of the worshipper to a temple. In South India, the medieval Hindu arts thrived under the patronage of the great dynasties since the Pallava period (6th–8th century), but also under the influence of the Vaishnavites (Alvars) and Shaivite (Nayanmar) itinerant saints who sang the praises of the gods through direct devotion, open to all social classes (*bhakti*). By bringing the deities out of the sanctuaries devoted to official Brahmin worship, with large processional floats or modest paintings by travelling storytellers, *bhakti* was an unprecedented phenomenon in India. It is not surprising that the folk arts – the source of the first cinematographic works – honoured Krishna and Rama. These avatars ('descents') of Vishnu, the hero of the *Mahabharata*[3] and *Ramayana*[4] epics, are the forms in which the supreme, celestial, and unattainable God incarnates to save the world and express a certain compassion.

3.
The *Mahabharata* ('The Great War of the Bharata' or 'Great Story of the Bharata') is a Sanskrit epic (itihasa) based on Hindu mythology. This very long epic poem was written between 3 BCE and 3 CE. It consists of some 100,000 stanzas (*sloka*), which amount to nearly 200,000 verses divided into 18 books. It is regarded as the greatest poem ever written. According to legend, it was composed by the god Ganesh and the sage Vyasa.

4.
The *Ramayana* ('Rama's Journey') is a mythological epic written in Sanskrit between 3 BCE and 3 CE. It consists of 7 chapters and 24,000 stanzas (48,000 verses). Like the *Mahabharata*, the *Ramayana* is one of the foundational texts of Hinduism and Hindu mythology. This poem is traditionally attributed to the legendary hermit Valmiki, and several regional versions exist.

5.
Diana L Eck, *Darśan, Seeing the Divine Image in India*, Columbia University Press, New York, 1996.

Alongside their transcendental forms housed in sanctuaries reserved for priests, the gods are able to act and approach the faithful. The staging of these mythologies in performing arts and later in cinema endows the action or 'divine performance' (*lila*) which is imbued with a beneficial power for the audience.

SEEING THE GODS

The magic in the early moving images of divinities does not lie solely with their link to the written mythological tradition (*purana*). It also originates from the power ascribed to the sight (*darshana*) of an image, place, or saint.[5] The concept of *darshan*, that is to say, the exchange of glances with a deity, powers the first mythological cinema. When Hindus visit a pilgrimage site or a temple, they receive *darshan*. Religious protection is achieved through sight, not only through prayers and rituals. It can also be the auspicious sight of charismatic religious figures such as ascetics or kings who formally appear to their subjects, as depicted in Mughal miniatures [cat. 27]. The crowd attending the return of the king of Mewar from England [fig. 1] seems driven by religious fervour.

The Nathadwara temple wall hanging [cat. 2], located in Rajasthan, depicts the moment when the Brahmins, responsible for overseeing religious worship, lower the curtains and illuminate the statue of Shri Nathji, the local form of Krishna, to offer the view to the faithful. The composition and the chromatic contrast of the face converge towards the eyes of the statue. The eyes are traditionally painted or carved last, during the 'eye-opening' ritual conducted by the Brahmins. The image can then be inhabited by the god who will have to be fed, entertained, and adorned to remain in residence.

This quest for closeness to the divine in popular culture contributed to the craze for the first mass-produced polychrome images inexpensively printed in the 1890s by Ravi Varma, a Travancore court portraitist, who painted in oil in the Western-style. He illustrated mythological

Cat. 1 Portable storyteller's shrine with panels of the Ramayana scenes. Rajasthan, India, mid-20th century. Painted wood. 33.5 × 22 × 20 cm. Paris, Musée du Quai Branly – Jacques Chirac, Inv. 71.1961.121.34.

Fig. 1 Anonymous. *The Return from England of the Maharaja of Jaipur, 4 November 1910*. Rajasthan, India, 1910. Aristotype print. 20 × 28 cm. Paris, Musée du Quai Branly – Jacques Chirac, Inv. PP0022638

texts in a naturalistic and dramatic way using oleography, a reproduction process introduced to India by German printers at that time. Ravi Varma's pictures flooded the country and shaped pan-Indian iconography with images that are still reproduced today, images that had considerable influence on cinema.

A SINGING AND DANCING CINEMA

Indian civilisation boasts one of the world's richest musical traditions, which is believed to be of divine origin. The goddess of arts and poetry, Sarasvati, is depicted playing the *vina* [cat. 4], while Shiva can be seen as 'the king of dance' when he celebrates his victory over the demons and embodies the triple divine function of creating/sustaining/destroying the universe [fig. 2]. Krishna's dance with his female worshippers expresses a desire for liberating the individual soul through its union with the divine [cat. 3]. Dancing is also part of the entertainment offered to the gods, and in Hindu temples there is a room dedicated to dance called the *mandapa*.

From the 5th century onwards, the *Natya Shastra*, or 'dance treatise' attributed to Bharata, theorised about *rasa* (i.e., emotions or more literally 'flavours') and their expression through attitudes, gestures, and colours, which are found in both the performing and the visual arts.[6] Even when frozen in a posture in a painting or sculpture, the gods adopt canonical dance attitudes and gestures. The *Natya Shastra* considers four primordial *rasas*: erotic, furious, heroic, and grotesque, all of which will form an artistic and dramatic language that will influence the actors' choreography and acting.

When cinema was introduced, it relied on the knowledge of the mythological repertoire in two ways: figurative, on the one hand, through statues and visual arts, and on the other hand, theatrical and musical. The *Ramayana* and *Mahabharata* epics, which have been massively performed by travelling theatre companies, have been known for more than two thousand years and are still being adapted into films and TV series. These myths form a genuine and continuous common thread in the great book of Indian history.

6.
John Guy, *Indian Temple Sculpture*, London, V&A Publications, 2007.

7.
Silver screen refers to black and white films in this context.

SUPERSTARS: THE GODS OF CINEMA

Dadasaheb Phalke made his first films based on mythological texts and lithographs from Ravi Varma's printing presses, where he had started his career. From the 1920s to the 1940s, an entire film industry was created and developed around major studios such as Himanshu Rai's Bombay Talkies and the Prabhat Film Company in North India. In the early 1950s, the large studios collapsed and made way for a system that is still prevalent today. This new system focuses on the star of the film, who is the key to its success. The productions had separated themselves from the mythological genre, but still attempted to build a national identity even within the films where their cinematic language developed. Themes, staging, narrative forms, and temporalities continued to evolve by becoming regional and intertwined with European cinema. The flourishing of the various regional industries outside Bombay undermined the dream of a unified, national cinema. The Bengali, Telugu, Tamil, Marathi, and Malayalam industries organised themselves and, a few years later, gave birth to the creation of a plethora of 'woods': Kollywood (Kodambakkam), Tollywood (Hyderabad) and Mollywood (Trivandrum) in the South, as well as Tollywood (Tollygunge) in Bengal.

The 1950s saw the dawn of a lavish golden age where the kings and queens of the silver screen[7] shone in breath-taking melodramas. Guru Dutt, Raj Kapoor [fig. 3], and Mehboob Khan [fig. 13 and fig. 14] were among the most glamorous representatives of the Hindi industry. During the same period, an Indian-style neorealism emerged with Bimal Roy. Trained at the school of large studios at the New Theatre, Calcutta, he paved the way for the realist and social 'Parallel Cinema', of which Satyajit Ray [cat. 35] would become the most prominent representative a few years later.

The 1950s also brought the era of the star system. Actors gained in popularity and became increasingly prolific. Paid on a fee basis, they would play in one film in the morning and in another one in the afternoon. From then on, the audience went to the cinema to see the star rather than for the story, director, or genre. Film heroes and heroines have replaced mythological ones, becoming demigods and goddesses venerated in the darkness of the cinema.

Cat. 2 *The Offering of the 'Food Mountain'* (annakuta) *to Krishna Shri Nathji*. Temple wall hanging (*pichhwai*). Nathadwara, Rajasthan, India, 19th century. Painting on cotton canvas. 254 × 237 cm. Paris, Musée du Quai Branly – Jacques Chirac, Inv. 70.2014.10.1

Worshippers bring numerous dishes to Shri Nathji, the local form of Krishna. The Brahmins lower the curtains of the shrine to enable *darshan* – the exchange of glances between the god and his worshippers.

Cat. 3 *Krishna Dancing with the Cowherd Girls* (rasa lila). Temple wall
hanging (*pichhwai*). Nathadwara, Rajasthan, India, 19th century. Painting
on cotton canvas. 251.5 × 268 cm. Paris, Musée du Quai Branly – Jacques Chirac,
Inv. 70.2016.10.1

Krishna dances with his female worshippers on the banks of the holy river
Yamuna. The multiple depictions of Krishna represent the love for the
alluring god who occupies the minds of the cowherd girls. This kaleidoscopic
composition is commonly seen in dance sequences in Indian films.

Cat. 4 *Sarasvati, The Goddess of Arts and Poetry.* North India, c. 1980. Chromolithograph adorned with fabric, beads, sequins, and gold thread. 52 × 37.5 cm. Paris, Musée du Quai Branly – Jacques Chirac, Inv. 71.1981.59.105.10.

Fig. 2 *Dancing Shiva (nataraja).* South India, c. 950–1000. Bronze. 83 × 47.5 × 24.5 cm.
Abu Dhabi, Louvre Abu Dhabi, LAD 2009.023

Cat. 5 *The Demon King Ravana*. Chhau Dance Mask. Purulia, West Bengal, India, c. 1990. Painted and varnished papier mâché. 38.5 × 101 × 18 cm. Paris, Musée du Quai Branly – Jacques Chirac, Inv. 71.1996.28.1.

Cat. 7 Jaba Chitrakar. *The 2007 Tsunami*. Storyteller painting on a scroll. Bengal, India, 2007. Pigments on paper, cotton canvas, and wood. 345 × 57 cm. Paris, Musée du Quai Branly – Jacques Chirac (gift of Catherine Clément), Inv. 70.2007.37.2

Cat. 8   *Hanuman, General of the Monkey Army*. Tamil Nadu, India, 19th century. Bronze. 34 × 12.5 × 13 cm.
Paris, Musée National des Arts Asiatiques – Guimet, Inv. MG811

Cat. 9 *Princess Sita Under a Tree*. Shadow-puppet (*tholubommalata*). Andhra Pradesh, India, first half of the 20th century. Painted buckskin. 97 × 71 cm. Paris, Musée du Quai Branly - Jacques Chirac, Inv. 71.1967.25.47

Cat. 10 *Krishna Surrounded by Gopis*. Mewar, Rajasthan, India, c. 1655. Pigments, gold, and silver on paper. 14.7 × 17 cm. Abu Dhabi, Louvre Abu Dhabi, LAD 2011.037

Fig. 3 Poster for the film *Rain* (*Barsaat*, 1949), directed by Raj Kapoor. Collection Sally and François Picard

Next double page Cat. 11 Stills from *Shiraz* (1928), directed by Franz Osten

RAJ KAPOOR'S

BARSAAT

Blinded by years of tears and by the shock of his beloved's death, Shiraz strives to give form to his memories — his love.

'Your work is finished, Shiraz. Henceforth this shall be known as Taj Mahal, in memory of her we both have loved.'

'With its nested plots, magical weapons, fantastic animals, and superhuman feats, Indian mythology is a birthplace of extraordinarily epic imaginary and provides a perennial and never-ending source of inspiration.'

A Kaleidoscope of Mythological Images

AMANDINE D'AZEVEDO

MYTHOLOGY AS A COMMON SPACE

Suddenly, Krishna rose from the water on the head of the snake-demon Kaliya! In the foreground, the villagers raised their hands in amazement at the miracle: the child-god has defeated the demon and now stands proudly above the waves.

In cinema, a new fervour has gripped hearts – the divinity appears in front of everyone: the film not only reveals the god, but he is moving and watching us [cat. 12]. Directed by Dadasaheb Phalke, who is considered the 'father of Indian cinema', *Kaliya Mardan* (1919) was one of the first films to project the miracles of Hindu mythology onto the big screen. Talkies would later provide the audience with long musical sequences, including religious chants and devotional music. Then, from the 1940s onwards, the moving images had colours that would tint Krishna's skin a beautiful indigo hue, and the jewellery worn by the goddesses would sparkle in gold. Popular cinemas and all the film industries from the north to the south of the country serve as favoured, unique, and powerful vehicles for Indian mythology. Cinematic techniques, such as superimposition and slow motion, became tools used to recount the magic and the exploits of the gods and goddesses.

However, this link between cinema and mythology draws its energy from many other visual forms that are both ancient and contemporary to the birth of Indian cinema, which is only one facet of the multiple encounters between the gods and the image.

In India, mythology is a prolific territory, known as much for its stories as its aesthetics. The great epics and myths have been narrated in a variety of forms, and for a very long time in theatre, painting, poetry, and songs. With its nested plots, magical weapons, fantastic animals, and superhuman feats, Indian mythology is a birthplace of extraordinarily epic imaginary and provides a perennial and never-ending source of inspiration with family betrayals, divine interventions, incredible escapes, and twists of fate that follow one after another. The intervention of the monkey god Hanuman to save Princess Sita is still one of the most famous episodes of the *Ramayana*, while the game of dice between rival cousins in the *Mahabharata* is constantly depicted and re-enacted in everything from miniatures to poetry, architectural friezes to comics. Mythological stories offer a framework for thought and action with adventure stories punctuated by philosophical, moral, and spiritual interludes. This mythology remains alive in society within arts and popular culture, for it is always invoked through words and images. Far from being confined and controlled by the clergy or the temples, the images of the gods are made of hybrid composites and are not hidden or reserved for a privileged few. In fact, they are for everyone.

The vortex-like place where most of the images arise is the bazaar. Located in the heart of the city, the bazaar escapes and reshapes identities by being, at the same time, a platform for trade and exchange; a religious and political space; and a meeting point between the colonial world and a vernacular structure.

In this space, images flow in and then flow out, transformed. In the bazaar, no form remains unchanged.

CUT/PASTE: THE DIVINE MOBILITY

Initially intended to decorate colonial interiors, when German lithographs – representations of snowy landscapes, Swiss chalets or Italian lakes – reached India they were an immediate hit, not only limited to their initial targeted clientele. Originally, the landscapes were devoid of figures and are often quite austere, but the newer embellished reinterpretations had additions in the form of 'collaged' Indian gods. Now, Krishna plays the flute by a lake and Shiva meditates in a snowy forest, while peacocks take advantage of the shade under the trees... All of the figures from Indian mythology had come to populate the empty and decorative European landscapes [fig. 8].

This art of collage, which combines different modes of representation and imagination, places the gods against a foreign backdrop, long before cinema did the same, by sending its heroes to dance in the world's most iconic places. While Bollywood and Kollywood stars dance in front of the Eiffel Tower, the Brooklyn Bridge, or Machu Picchu, the collages on the lithographs, that arrived from Europe at the beginning of the 20th century, had already anticipated these journeys, as well as the heterogeneity between the Indian stories and characters against their foreign and exotic backgrounds. Europe had become an exotic and fantasised place with its Swiss snow-covered mountain peaks and lush valleys. Imaginations intertwined as much as techniques did.

This direct intervention on the images, to adapt them to local taste, escaped any predefined composition. According to Sumathi Ramaswamy, 'No visual image is self-sufficient, bounded, insulated; instead, it is open, porous, permeable, and even available for appropriation.'[1] This appropriation turns images, especially divine representations, into a place of sharing, since they belong to no one and circulate everywhere, on all media and in all contexts.

1.
Sumathi Ramaswamy, director, *Beyond Appearances? Visual Practices and Ideologies in Modern India*, New Delhi/ Thousand Oaks, Sage, 2003, introduction, p. xvi.

DISSEMINATING IMAGES ACROSS THE LAND

Collages aren't the only invention of the bazaar. Advertisements were posted on the walls of shops and in the streets, promoting Vinolia soap, Parle-G biscuits, Woodward's medicine, or the oil company Burmah-Shell, for example. These consumer products were advertised with the gods: as if Krishna as a child defeated the snake Kaliya, but suddenly, he *also* did so thanks to Burmah-Shell petrol! [fig. 4]. Or the goddesses with their delicate skin unfailingly praising the softness of a fragrant soap... This blurring of the lines between the divine and the mass image was to some extent due to the very famous painter Ravi Varma, who was one of the first to portray the Hindu pantheon in a naturalistic way, thanks to his mastery of Western artistic techniques like depicting volume, chiaroscuro, and painting in oil. By launching his own lithographic press, he flooded the pan-Indian world with his representations of gods and goddesses. While his oil paintings were hardly known beyond the privileged circles of his collectors and the art fairs, his reproductions reached every household. His images would soon decorate everything from calendars and advertisements to the tiniest matchbox. Images of deities by Varma were very popular and circulated relentlessly throughout the country, passing from hand to hand, especially in the form of calendars. These were then often augmented: decorated with beads, pieces of silk attached to costumes, and sequins directly embroidered onto the paper. It wasn't unusual to surround the frame with fresh flowers and to apply sandalwood paste on the auspicious figures' foreheads. A contemporary to the birth of cinema, Varma's art represents a key lineage for the early films of Phalke (who also worked at Varma's print workshop) or for those of Baburao Painter, which featured the gods [fig. 5 and fig. 6].

Varma provided Indian deities with a visual canon, and a body, while cinema brought them to life. In the 1920s, most of the country's film production – about 70% – was based on mythological and religious stories, and it is fascinating to see how the postures and costumes of the films seem to come straight out of a Varma painting. Therefore, it could be said that a painter invented Indian mythological cinema!

Dreaming of seeing the gods in motion and never being satisfied with their fixed and distant image, was what encouraged people to

Fig. 4   Advertising calendar for Burmah-Shell
petrol. 1939. Chromolithograph. 52 × 44 cm.
Priya Paul Collection

Cat. 12   Krishna's victory in *Kaliya Mardan* (1919),
directed by Dadasaheb Phalke

Fig. 5   Yashoda and Krishna in *Muraliwala* (1927), directed by Baburao Painter

Fig. 6   Ravi Varma (1848–1906). *Go-dohana*. Undated. Chromolithograph. 35.6 × 25.4 cm.
Bangalore, Collection of the Sandeep & Gitanjali Maini Foundation

get closer to them. On the street, one may stumble upon a peculiar optical toy called a bioscope. For more than one hundred years, this object has been surrounded by crowds of children anxious to peer through the various windows arranged along the side of the box.

With this very rudimentary object (which was also found in China, and Iran under the name of *shahre farang*), one can slide images, often with the help of a crank similar to a music box. The latest bioscopes also include mini video projectors or even DVD players! However, the idea remains the same: to put one's head against the viewfinder and watch. Much could be said about this constant desire to see and share images, about how an optical toy keeps evolving year after year without ever disappearing completely. But why would anyone continue to look through a bioscope if cinema and television exist? Perhaps because this little box travels, bringing images to pedestrians on the street, just like a salesman offering precisely what one desires. The bioscope display prolongs the proximity to the image, its popular nature, and the fleeting and affordable pleasure of peering inside a picture box.

THE GODS OF THE MAGIC LANTERN

The magic lantern is another medium that is virtually invisible and forgotten in India, but also must be taken into account. Originating in 17th-century Europe, this simple device is a light source inside a box that projects a transparent image placed in front of a magnifying lens onto a surface (usually a wall or a screen). Painted on glass, the images are projected by sliding them in front of the light source. In the history of technology and media, the magic lantern is often referred to as a kind of pre-cinematic object, because it almost disappeared after the advent of cinema. These two technologies share many common features: projection, music, and a narrative accompanying the images. When the magic lantern was brought to India by the British, it was mainly used for educational and religious purposes: it was a medium for promulgating hygiene, explaining agricultural principles, or was even used by missionaries to present their religion. However, the magic lantern was bound to have a different history in India. The vernacular adaptation and magical reinterpretation turned this colonial object into a vehicle for Indian imagery. Only one copy

2.
A popular form of Bengali painting, still alive today, that consists of a painted scroll of images bound in boxes. As the scroll unfolds, its presenter narrates the adventures depicted.

has survived of this narrative-based and mythological Indian lantern, preserved by the National Film Archive of India. Its inventor and first operator, Mahadeo Gopal Patwardhan, attended a magic lantern show at the end of the 19th century and immediately grasped the advantages of proposing a more local and fictional version of the very same object. Embarking on the venture with his friend, M M Pitale, the two of them undertook the production of a magic lantern, which Patwardhan would later modify. Upon his demise, his sons Vinayak Mahadeo and Ramchandra, operated the Indian magic lantern under the name of the Patwardhan Brothers from 1892 to 1918, well after the emergence of cinema in India. Rather than just offering still images, the brothers chose to animate them by ingeniously superimposing several glass plates. By sliding the mechanism, the plates would overlap and create movement. During the projections, the heroes would raise their arms, their lips would move, and miracles would unfold...

Why is this object so important when so few of them remain? In fact, the surviving lantern plates are dazzling, with images such as Krishna watching women bathing amidst the foliage by the water, or the goddess Sarasvati parading around on a peacock that is spreading its tail. Several plates feature dancers in a row with their arms raised and their skirts richly adorned with motifs. The Indian magic lantern has its very own hybrid language, somewhere between the still images of the bazaar and the moving images of cinema. Thus, it would be a pity to consider the lantern as just a mere pre-cinematic object [fig. 7].

The printed images of the bazaar, bioscope, or even the magic lantern, recount a visual field in which cinema isn't a technological outcome, but rather a close relative of all these objects and visual practices. The forms of cinema and its images share much in common with these (re)inventions, and European objects became part of the long history of narrating and showing Indian myths. As Researcher Sudhir Mahadevan explains, 'An already richly constituted field of visual practices preceded cinema's arrival and shaped its cultural meanings and socio-political functions. Personnel and iconography crossed over freely between the painted, printed, photographic, and moving image, between urban commercial theatre and other proto-cinematic arts such as the Kalighat scroll paintings.[2]

An already 'inter-ocular' field shaped cinema, not the other way around.'[3]

The images circulate and are exchanged, none of them belonging to any medium in particular. This 'interocularity' re-enacts what has been said about the life of texts – intertextuality – which refuses to isolate an idea or a story in order to expose its network and influence. In India, images and mediums are reborn in each other, subdued only to come back better later, as if Krishna as a child, so moving, in the 1919 film image had simply leapt onto the screen from the magic lantern plate, bioscope slide, or bazaar collage. As an oral and visual tradition, cinema is a fragment of a dense visual field that evolves and combines pieces, producing as much as it reactivates the visual culture that precedes it, and which enriches it in return.

It is then necessary to consider the etymology and the principle of the title of this text, the kaleidoscope, which is a set of mirrors that, endlessly, brings together forms to create images. Not just any images, but ones that are: *kalós* (beautiful), *eîdos* (aspect) and *skopéô* (to observe). This active gaze towards beautiful forms, which constantly catch the light, disappearing and reappearing, tells us something about Indian imagery, which is alive and always accessible.

3.
Sudhir Mahadevan, 'Early Cinema in South Asia: The Place of Technology in Narrative of its Emergence', *Framework*, vol. 54, no 2, Autumn 2013, p. 141.

Fig. 7 *The Snake Vasuki Protecting Baby Krishna*. Plate of a Patwardhan magic lantern.
Produced by Vinayak Mahadeo Patwardhan. c. 1900. Approx. 10 × 25.5 cm. Pune, National Film Archive of India

Fig. 8 Collage Representing Krishna. c. 1930. Paper cut-outs glued on a chromolithograph.
49 × 70 cm. Private collection

'Varma's lithographs began to tell a story about the birth of the Indian nation, where a certain idea of India emerges.'

Ravi Varma

HÉLÈNE KESSOUS

Ravi Varma Koil Thampuran (1848–1906) was born into a large family in Travancore, a princely state in southern India. His family descended from a *kshatriya* (warrior) caste but renounced fighting to dedicate themselves to art, philosophy, and Sanskrit studies. His maternal uncle was a painter and his mother was a music composer, in addition to being an Ayurvedic practitioner. Ravi Varma grew up in the Court of Travancore and according to legend, he was only talented at drawing as a student. Renowned within his family for his style, he is said to have decorated the walls of the family house with drawings made from a piece of charcoal from the kitchen.

Ravi Varma first came into contact with European painting at the Travancore court. Indeed, the British Painter Theodore Jensen visited the court in 1868 in search of portrait commissions. He did not properly teach Varma oil painting but would let him watch while he worked. Varma was already an accomplished painter, but his aristocratic origins hindered him from becoming a professional painter. It was only in 1870, while meditating on the patron goddess of his clan, that Varma decided to devote himself to painting. His first work was a family portrait entitled *Khizzhake Menon and his Family*. From the outset of his career, he developed two visual languages. The first one dealt with exotic paintings aimed at Western collectors, while the other was characterised by a lavish and flamboyant aesthetic for the luxurious tastes of the Indian aristocracy and bourgeoisie. While the West would soon replace painted portraits with photographs,

1.
Erwin Neumayer and Christine Schelberger, *Popular Indian Art: Raja Ravi Varma and the Printed Gods of India*, New Delhi, Oxford University Press, 2003, p. 39–40 .

in India, the local aristocratic families replaced traditional Mughal-style portraits with oil paintings [**fig. 10 and cat. 14***]. Varma's portraits were not just simple depictions of family life, but what appealed to his commissioners was to be represented alongside their tutelary gods and goddesses, who are inseparable from Indian life.

Shortly afterwards, Varma was commissioned to redecorate the Mysore Palace, for which he was asked to paint a series of deities. At this moment, the trend for mythological scenery was born and would go on to conquer the rest of India. During his career as a commissioned painter, Varma shaped his world and aesthetics to become an established artist in 1890, twenty years after he began. Stylistically, his chromolithographs provided a compelling reinterpretation of European Orientalism, but made by an 'Oriental' artist[1].

Varma's art draws inspiration from many sources, such as illustrated books and posters advertising European products in Indian markets. However, the cheap chromolithographs, which Germany exported in such large quantities that they were commonly referred to as 'German prints', are believed to have been his most decisive influence. When setting up his printing studio, Varma chose to use German industrial equipment, and years later, a German would take over its operation.

Printing for the Indian market was nothing new: until then, artists designed and sent the models to Europe to be lithographed. By locating his press operations in India to produce high-quality prints of his mythological paintings, Varma's venture was a daring one. From then on, his project took on a political dimension and his work became a showcase for the rise of national consciousness, a means for restoring the grandeur of cultural heritage, and for empowering the country. The normative power of his iconography paved the way for Hindu pan-Indian imagery [fig. 9 and cat. 13]. Varma's lithographs began to tell a story about the birth of the Indian nation, where a certain idea of India emerges. In his paintings, Varma's heroes call for an uprising, for the repossession of cultural and traditional values that had been undermined and diminished for centuries by British colonisation. In a similar attempt to instil nationalistic sentiments, the light colour of the complexions in Varma's paintings glorifies a mythological past. It is unclear whether this whitening was intended to convince Westerners of the mythical and glorious aspects of this past or, on the contrary, to convince the Indians themselves. The allegorical complexion of the skin, the whiteness that emanates from Ravi Varma's works, despite his naturalistic style,[2] was not meant to mirror reality, but rather to depict a fantasy world. And this fantasy world, where gods appear alongside humans, would be staged and set in motion by the cinema.

2.
According to his detractors Varma's naturalism, thought of as specific to Western painting, undermined the perceived dedication to Indian heritage in his work. See: Kajri Jain, Gods in the Bazaar: The Economies of Indian Calendar Art, Duke University Press, Durham, 2007.

Fig. 9   Ravi Varma (1848–1906). *Radha and Krishna*. Undated. Oil on canvas. 69.85 × 59.7 cm. Private collection

आदि लक्ष्मी

SOLE AGENTS:- E.G.KRISHNIAH SETTY & SON.
Avenue Road, Bangalore City.

ADI LAXMI.

Copy right Registered No. 3.
RAVI-VARMA-PRESS. MALAVLI-LONAVLI.

Cat. 13   After G V Venkatesh (active in the 1920s), *Lakshmi, Goddess of Fortune*. North India, early 20th century.
Chromolithograph adorned with fabric, beads, sequins, and gold thread. 54.2 × 39 × 1.5 cm.
Paris, Musée du Quai Branly – Jacques Chirac, Inv. 75.2012.0.689

Since their creation by Ravi Varma's studios, printed religious images have been ubiquitous in India. The embellished
images are adorned with garments and jewellery – just like temple sculptures. Early Indian cinema directly
transposed the naturalistic and dramatic compositions of these images.

Fig. 10   Ravi Varma (1848–1906). *The Coquette*. Undated. Oil on canvas. 74.9 × 58.4 cm. Private collection

Cat. 14*   Ravi Varma (1848–1906). *Woman Holding a Fan*. c. 1895. Oil on canvas.
53.5 × 35.9 cm. London, Victoria & Albert Museum

'Phalke drew inspiration from the deep cultural and religious roots of the subcontinent, which influenced the direction of his films and created a genre that would be immediately successful: mythological films.'

Dadasaheb Phalke

HÉLÈNE KESSOUS

Dhundiraj Govind Phalke (1870–1944) is considered the father of Indian cinema. Affectionately nicknamed Dadasaheb Phalke, he was a pioneer in many respects. As the first professional in Indian cinema, he also embodied a refined and politically conscious Indian elite who considered cinema to be essential in identity construction and national awakening. A fervent supporter of the Swadheshi movement, a nationalist movement that advocated a 'made in India' approach and rejected anything that came from abroad, he was soon convinced that Indian cinema should be directed by Indians and made for Indians.

While India was still under British rule, there was much at stake in the creation of this national film industry. Cinema faced a huge challenge: how to appeal to everyone despite the different languages and cultures? To do so, Phalke drew inspiration from the deep cultural and religious roots of the subcontinent, which influenced the direction of his films and created a genre that would be immediately successful: mythological films.

Phalke descended from a family of Brahmins from Maharashtra (Bombay region). Endowed with a solid foundation in classical culture, he was a scholar with an excellent knowledge of Sanskrit and classical literature. Phalke was polymath with a profound passion for images and experimented with different artistic talents such as photography, ceramics, illusionism, magic, and even editioned art. It was as if, without knowing it, he was preparing himself to be the ingenious director that he would become a few years later. Undoubtedly, the encounter with Ravi Varma [cat. 15] was one of the most decisive moments of his early years. Indeed,

Phalke worked for almost ten years in the painter-lithographer's studio. Thus, it is not surprising that his filmography reflects the unique style of the famous printing workshop that revolutionised Indian imagery by flooding the market with stylised lithographs. It was only after these experiences that Phalke found his way into the burgeoning art of cinematography.

According to legend, in 1910–1911, while watching Alice Guy's *The Birth, the Life and the Death of Christ* (1906, fig. 11), which was being screened in a Bombay (present-day Mumbai) cinema for Easter, Phalke got the idea of adapting this film genre to the Indian context. After all, if the West could stage its god, why couldn't the Indians do the same? India and Hinduism are brimming with stories and legends based on a pantheon full of deities. Above all, as he thought at the time, this heritage was common to a majority of Indians. Thus, he decided to become a filmmaker and adapt the great Hindu epics to film. After investing in second-hand gear he found in India and shooting a few short films to gain experience, he decided to embrace a professional career. Without wasting any more time, he travelled to London in 1912 to buy equipment and familiarise himself with the latest technological breakthroughs. Back in India, he dedicated himself fully to his project and involved those around him. For instance, it was his wife who developed the films on the ground floor of their house. Very shortly afterwards, he directed India's first fiction feature-length film, entitled *Raja Harishchandra*. The film was released in Bombay on 21 April 1913 and was a commercial success that received critical acclaim. A second version of the same film, *Satyavadi*

Harishchandra, was completed in 1917 [cat. 18]. The story is drawn from the *Mahabharata*, and features a good king who sacrifices everything – power, wife, and child – for the sake of justice, and who is rewarded by the gods who are moved by such self-sacrifice. In the early days of Indian cinema, women's roles were played by men, but Phalke soon changed this practice and featured women in his second film, *Mohini Bhasmasur* (The Legend of Bhasmasur), which was released that same year.

Choosing to exclusively shoot films based on Indian stories was risky, since he wanted to create a profitable domestic industry. In doing so, he moved away from the anglicised Indian population to focus on a broader audience. With 27 short films and 95 feature-length films under his belt, Phalke was a prolific filmmaker.

He first introduced the mythological genre with *Raja Harishchandra*, which was to become an early milestone for the Indian film industry. Back in Phalke's time, the confusion between the gods themselves and the gods featured in the films was so great that it was not unusual for the audience to show their devotion by praying when they appeared on the screen. This is something that is still done today, whenever the film stars – the new gods – appear on the screen. With the film *Raja Harishchandra*, Phalke created an unwavering bond between mythological stories, gods, and cinema, granting Indian cinema a special place in the hearts of believers.

Concise filmography:
Raja Harishchandra (1913)
Mohini Bhasmasur (1913)
Satyavan Savitri (1914)
Lanka Dahan (*Lanka Aflame*, 1917)
Satyavadi Harishchandra (1917) [cat. 18]
Shri Krishna Janma (*The Birth of Shree Krishna*, 1918)
Kaliya Mardan (The Childhood of Krishna, 1919) [cat. 12 and cat. 17]
Buddhadev (1923)
Setu Bandhan (Bridging the Ocean, 1932)
Gangavataran (1937)

Fig. 11   *The Birth, the Life and the Death of Christ* (1906), directed by Alice Guy, which inspired Phalke

Fig. 12   Dadasaheb Phalke

REGISTERED N° 190   अनंतशिवाजीदेसाई   राधाकृष्ण.   मोतीबाजार मुंबई.   RAVI·VARMA·PRESS·KARLA·LONAVLA

Cat. 15 Ravi Varma (1848–1906). *Krishna Declaring His Love for Radha Via a Confidante.* After 1900.
Chromolithograph. 71 × 50.8 cm. Private collection

Cat. 16   Statuette of Krishna. Rajasthan, second half of the 19th century. Painted marble. 50.5 × 17.5 × 13 cm.
Paris, Musée du Quai Branly – Jacques Chirac, Inv. 71.1930.54.471 D

The god Krishna experiences the life of a humble peasant and can either be represented as a mischievous child or as a charming young man. Since he is close to his worshippers, Krishna is highly revered, which contributes to the fact that he became one of the first heroes celebrated in cinema.

Cat. 17   Krishna as a child playing the flute in *Kaliya Mardan* (1919), directed by Dadasaheb Phalke

Cat. 18 *Satyavadi Harishchandra* (1917),
directed by Dadasaheb Phalke

The Emperor Shah Jahan (Charu Roy) and Shiraz (Himanshu Rai) in *Shiraz* (1928),
directed by Franz Osten (see cat. 11, pages 42–43 and cat. 19, page 78)

India
in Cinema

'Indian cinema's dream
of a unitary country
is presented best in the
subgenre of historical
drama.'

Rajputs and Mughals in Bollywood: India's Fantasised History

OPHÉLIE WIEL

In 1947, India gained its independence, but to the great despair of the revered hero of the anti-colonial fight, Mahatma Gandhi, the former British Empire was partitioned over religious lines, leading to the emergence of the new state of Pakistan. The crisscrossing exodus of Hindus and Muslims resulted in hundreds of thousands of casualties. India and Pakistan became intimate enemies, and Muslims became a minority group that is sometimes discriminated against in Hindu territory.

At the same time, Muslim Filmmaker Mehboob Khan left his Bombay (present-day Mumbai) studio and reached the Pakistani border, before he turned back, perhaps intuitively knowing that, as Mihir Bose explains, 'Most of the Muslim [artists] who went to the new state vanished without trace.'[1] In 1945, Mehboob Khan directed *Humayun* [fig. 13 and fig. 14], an ode to community harmony, in line with the philosophy of the Bollywood industry. Mihir Bose explained: 'Bollywood [had long created] an India that was very different to the real India outside. Here, none of the bitterness and divide between the two great religious communities occurred [...]. In the India of Bollywood, Hindus fell in love with Muslims and even married them, as it was quite common for Muslim actors and actresses to play Hindu characters.'[2]

A CINEMA IN SEARCH OF AN ELUSIVE NATIONAL UNITY

Indian cinema's dream of a unitary country is presented best in the subgenre of historical drama. It is, indeed, a subgenre, since spectacular epics recounting India's rich past constitute only a small fraction of Bombay cinema's considerable production: the Mughal period, for example (the most documented historical period), accounts for no more than forty films, from the 1920s until today. The prohibitive cost of these films is a factor; however, the most successful ones were big box-office hits, for instance, *Mughal-e-Azam* (1960) by K Asif [fig. 15] remained the most lucrative film in history for fifteen years.

However, which 'history' are we talking about? In a country that avoids the most sensitive subjects, which are likely to ignite latent tensions, the Mughal Empire is seen as a golden age. The Mughals were invaders that came from present-day Uzbekistan. While they were not the first Muslims to rule the subcontinent, they instilled in people's minds, and over time (from 1526 to 1858, even if the empire went into decline from 1707 onwards), that this was a period of religious tolerance that Bollywood would later seek to echo. Contemporary India has absorbed part of this heritage. At the time of Emperor Humayun (16th century), the Hindi language, spoken colloquially, acquired Persian-Arabic influences, which gave rise to the very similar languages: Hindustani (Devanagari alphabet) and Urdu (Arabic alphabet). These were the languages used in the film industry in 20th-century Bombay. Urdu allows for highly prized flights of lyricism, as shown in, for instance, according to Theorist Ashis Nandy, 'the characters of *Mughal-e-Azam* [that] do not just speak – they refine communication, they distil it, they crystallise it into many-faceted glittering gems, they make poetry of ordinary language.'[3]

1.
Mihir Bose, *Bollywood: A History*, Delhi, Roli Books, 2007, p. 196.

2.
Ibid., p. 190.

THE MUGHAL MUSLIM EMPIRE: AN OBJECT OF FANTASY

In a country with a Hindu majority,[4] such enthusiasm for the Muslim coloniser may seem paradoxical. However, in more precise terms, this is not about colonisation, at least not from a European perspective. In the Mughal Empire, Hindu subjects were allowed to observe their own customs and obey their own laws, as long as they paid the *jizya*, a special tax on non-Muslims, later abolished by Akbar. It is worth pointing out that the most controversial monarch, Aurangzeb, who tried to enforce Sharia law across the subcontinent, is the least featured historical character in films. Conversely, Jalaluddin Muhammad 'Akbar' (translated as 'the Great'), the champion of tolerance, is portrayed in a significant number of films, even if he is not necessarily the leading character. For example, he is featured in the multiple versions of the legend *Anarkali* (1928, 1935, 1953, and *Mughal-e-Azam* in 1960), in *Jodhaa Akbar* (2008) by Ashutosh Gowariker [fig. 17], or even in *Humayun*, in which he appears as a child after his parents' wedding. The revolts started by his son Salim, the monarch known as Jehangir, were turned into more acceptable rebellions by Bollywood, because they were driven by impossible love (*Anarkali*, again, but also *Noor Jehan* directed in 1967 by Muhammad Sadiq). Lastly, Shah Jahan, the son of Jehangir, who built the symbol of India, the iconic Taj Mahal, for his beloved wife Mumtaz Mahal, is also one of Bollywood's favourite romantic characters, as seen in the silent film *Shiraz* (1928) by Franz Osten [cat. 11 and cat. 19], but also in *Mumtaz Mahal* (Kidar Nath Sharma, 1944), *Taj Mahal* (M Sadiq, 1963) or *Taj Mahal: An Eternal Love Story* (Akbar Khan, 2005).

Above all, Bollywood emphasises the legendary justice of the Mughals in spectacular and magnificent palaces: Akbar's gigantic 'scales of justice' appears in *Mughal-e-Azam*, where it becomes the focus of a moral lesson from the father to his son Salim, who seems to show immoral propensities from childhood, as well as in *Jodhaa Akbar*, where the monarch is seated on a scale so that his Hindu subjects can prove their loyalty by counterbalancing his weight with goods from all over the country. In *Humayun*, Emperor Babur, founder of the Mughal dynasty, states that 'rich and poor are judged in the same way'. In *Noor Jehan*, immediately upon ascending

3.
Ashis Nandy, *The Secret Politics of Our Desires: Innocence, Culpability and Indian Popular Cinema*, London, Zed Books Ltd, 1999, p. 24.

4.
According to the last census conducted in 2011, close to 80% of Indians claimed to be Hindus, while 14% claimed to be Muslims.

the throne, Jehangir enacts social laws for the poor, and has a bell installed at the entrance of his palace, available to anyone who needs to call upon the monarch. Personally, he submits to the call of justice (religious justice, since he cannot be his own judge) when accused of murder by the woman he loves. Also presented are the terrible punishments awaiting offenders such as when Anarkali is immured alive in the 1953 film (Nandlal Jaswantlal); while the lover of Shah Jahan's favourite concubine risks having his head crushed by an elephant's foot in *Shiraz*.

Since the borders of present-day India are similar to the borders of Mughal India (at its largest expansion in 1707, with Aurangzeb's conquests), Bollywood could also create a nationalistic founding myth based on the Muslim empire. In films, Muslim rulers, though coming from abroad, are eager to profess their love and their feeling of belonging to 'Hindustan' (literally, 'land of the Hindus' in Persian). In *Jodhaa Akbar*, the monarch claims that 'this is [his] country' and a song makes him 'the life of Hindustan', while the mixing of colours in the costumes evoke the current Indian flag: white, green (the colour of Islam) and saffron (the colour of Hinduism and Buddhism).

The film *Mughal-e-Azam* stresses from the outset, using a voiceover on a map of India, that 'Akbar was among those who loved this land', and the plot revolves around the dilemma of the monarch, who must sacrifice his son to save his country.

THE AMBIGUOUS SYMBOLISM OF THE HINDU RAJPUTS

Rajputs ('sons of a king' in Sanskrit), the Hindu monarchs of northern India, stand out on the other side of the religious spectrum. Their roles are often secondary, even though Bollywood has recently tended to put them back in focus with *Jodhaa Akbar*, *Bajirao Mastani* (Sanjay Leela Bhansali, 2015), and *Padmaavat* (Sanjay Leela Bhansali, 2018, fig. 18). This is perhaps a sign of tension in the country's identity at a time when the 'unitary' Congress party is losing its footing against the considerable strength of the BJP, the Hindu nationalist party that has governed India since 2014. The Rajputs have been subject to historical contortions, for which cinema is not solely responsible. While they formed very

Fig. 13   Poster of *Humayun* (1945), directed by Mehboob Khan

Fig. 14   *Humayun* (1945), directed by Mehboob Khan

Fig. 15 Madhubala and Dilip Kumar in *Mughal-e-Azam* (1960), directed by K Asif

Cat. 19 Selima (Enakshi Rama Rao) and the Emperor Shah Jahan (Charu Roy) in *Shiraz* (1928), directed by Franz Osten

diverse clans since the 6th century CE (whose origins are much debated among historians), an elitist myth about them arose from the 16th–17th centuries onwards, which was later adopted by the English colonisers who identified them as counterparts to the medieval knights and then developed nationalist interpretations of the Rajput battles against the Mughal invaders.

Despite the rich diversity of Rajput kingdoms, Bollywood has chosen to essentialise them for the purpose of simplification with the sole division being whether they accepted Mughal rule. Indeed, many Rajput kingdoms had made alliances with the Mughals. For instance, Akbar had obtained their support to build his empire. The valorisation in the films of their legendary attributes, which came from Hindu epics, is even more interesting. These include: courage and physical strength ('A Rajput fights an enemy until his last breath', *Padmaavat*), dignity ('Rajputs are not used to being commanded', *Jodhaa Akbar*), honouring promises (*Mughal-e-Azam*) and a special skill in the handling of the sword. In fact, the gift and acceptance of the sword became the symbol of matrimonial alliance in *Bajirao Mastani*.

IMAGERY OF WOMEN: WARRIORS OR SAINTS?

These qualities are even celebrated amongst women: the Rajput patriarchal traditions (infanticide of daughters, *purdah*, – seclusion of women and hiding their bodies and faces – and *sati* – the immolation of widows on the funeral pyre of their husbands) all virtually disappear from the screen, while others are emphasised, such as polygamy in *Bajirao Mastani*, or *jauhar* – the collective immolation of women when an invader is about to capture them – in *Padmaavat*.

In cinema, Rajput women are praised for their 'courage', such as Mastani, who fights alongside Bajirao to save her kingdom; Padmavati, who declares that 'Rajput women are warriors equal to men'; or the soldierly Rajput princess, who challenges Emperor Babur at the beginning of *Humayun*, earning the admiration of the monarch. The qualities referred to as distinctively feminine, a leitmotif in Bollywood cinema, play a significant role in both Rajput and Mughal women: young girls are celebrated for their dignity and self-respect – such as the future Mumtaz Mahal in *Shiraz*, who only kneels before the prince 'of her own free will' – or for their virtue and devotion, like Mehrunisa in *Noor Jehan*, a widow who continues to defend the dignity of her murdered husband, and Hamida Bano in *Humayun*, who refuses the marriage proposal of the crown prince because she belongs to a lower social status.

FIGHTING RELIGIOUS INTOLERANCE

The relationship between the Rajputs and Mughals in Bombay cinema is not always peaceful, regardless of the importance given to religious differences, which can sometimes be conflated with the struggle for territorial domination – even though religious rites are often, together with costumes, the only way to distinguish people with similar physical characteristics. Conflicts are a plot twist that help to keep the action going, as in *Jodhaa Akbar*, where the emperor faces an alliance between a traitor from his own side and Rajput monarchs. However, it is noteworthy to say that the only Muslim monarch depicted as cruel and nearly insane is Alauddin (*Padmaavat*), who is not a Mughal, but descended from the Khilji, an Afghan dynasty that conquered the Delhi Sultanate in the 13th century. The Marathi, and therefore Hindu, *peshwa* (prime minister) in *Bajirao Mastani* can thereby explain that he is 'fighting against the Mughal dynasty, and not against their religion', and celebrates Eid with Mastani, his concubine, instead of going to a dinner organised for the Brahmin priests.

Religious tolerance, which even reached the point of syncretism in 1581 when Akbar promulgated the Din-i-Ilahi ('The Divine Faith', bringing together the Quran, Bible, and Hindu texts), still lies at the heart of the Bollywood vision, which above all values peaceful coexistence. Its best representative is still Akbar, whose trusted advisor, Raja Man Singh (a secondary character in many films) was his Hindu brother-in-law. Akbar married a Rajput princess, who became, from marriage, known as Mariam-uz-Zamani. She was not forced to become a Muslim and was able to keep her Hindu religion instead, which Bollywood is keen on showing through prayers and musical numbers dedicated to Krishna in *Jodhaa Akbar* or *Mughal-e-Azam*. In *Jodhaa Akbar*, they only use the princess' legendary first name, Jodhaa Bai (her real birth name is unknown), to further emphasise Akbar's eccentricity. Akbar explains that 'Respect for each other's religion will enrich Hindustan'. In the magic of cinema: Jodhaa not only becomes Akbar's favourite wife, but also his only wife (though like all Mughal rulers, he was known to be a polygamist).

CINEMA AS A REFUGE FROM THE DISILLUSIONMENT OF REALITY

However, it would be wrong to assume that Bombay cinema is overly political. In cinema, the feeling that prevails is neither patriotic nor religious. Love is still the essence of the Bollywood film 'formula' and enchants through the poetic and spectacular musical numbers. In *Humayun*, when Emperor Babur is about to die, his last words are that he wants his subjects to 'love each other like brothers'. In *Shiraz*, Shah Jahan refuses to use any kind of force to obtain the young slave girl he is in love with because he wants her to love him in return. In *Noor Jehan*, *Mughal-e-Azam*, and all versions of *Anarkali*, the crown prince, frustrated by his inability to marry the woman he desires, rebels against his father, and loses interest in his kingdom, to the point of nearly losing his life. In *Bajirao Mastani*, the *peshwa* is prepared to face his entire community to ensure that his concubine, rejected from the court because she is half Muslim, will eventually be accepted. Women also play an important role here, as they are the ones who, out of love, intervene in inter-religious or fratricidal battles, much like the Sabine women.

Where does the historical verisimilitude fit into all this? As noted, it has been repeatedly sacrificed. This should not be interpreted as history being disregarded, but in Bollywood, cinema is the ultimate space for dreams, fantasy, and imagination. The fact is that the crown Prince Salim did not rebel against his father Akbar for the beauty of a slave or a courtesan, but the legend of Anarkali ('pomegranate flower'), documented as early as the 16th century, is more likely to move a family audience to tears. The same applies to *Padmaavat*, inspired by a 16th-century epic, or *Bajirao Mastani*, based on a 1972 Marathi novel.

Influenced by real community tensions, Bombay's filmmakers engaged in a few preliminary warnings. At the beginning of *Jodhaa Akbar*, it is stated that the film offers 'one' version of the story. In *Anarkali* (1953), it is specified that it is a 'legend without historical foundation'. Director Sanjay Leela Bhansali, who has been dogged by attacks (sometimes physical) from both Hindu and Muslim communities, states at the beginning of *Padmaavat* and *Bajirao Mastani* that he does not intend to be 'faithful' to history, and that his films are respectful of 'all feelings and all communities...'.

This brings to mind the famous last line of John Ford's *The Man Who Shot Liberty Valance* (1962): 'When the legend becomes fact, print the legend'. In short, Bollywood's motto.

Cat. 20   Anonymous. *Rajput Prince*. India, 1910–1920. Photographic print with gouache highlights.
61 × 25.8 cm. Paris, Musée du Quai Branly – Jacques Chirac, Inv. 70.2019.34.4

chadjehan.

Cat. 21*   After Mir Hashim (active from 1620 to 1660)?, *Emperor Shah Jahan Holding an Iri*s. Mughal school, c. 1655.
Ink, pigments, and gold on paper. 45 × 32 cm. Paris, Bibliothèque Nationale de France, Prints and Photography Department,
Inv. Réserve OD-44, FOL, f. 27. Gift of Colonel Gentil, 1785. Cat. RH n°47

Fig. 16 *Princess Padmavati*. Faizabad, c. 1765. Gouache and gold on paper. 40.3 × 27.3 cm.
Paris, Bibliothèque Nationale de France, Prints and Photography Department, Inv. Réserve OD-43, PET FOL, f. 36.
Gift of Colonel Gentil

Fig. 17   Hrithik Roshan and Aishwarya Rai in *Jodhaa Akbar* (2008), directed by Ashutosh Gowariker

Fig. 18 Deepika Padukone and Shahid Kapoor in *Padmaavat* (2018), directed by Sanjay Leela Bhansali

Cat. 22   Johnston & Hoffman (photographers active from 1880–1950). *The Udaipur Maharaja's Assembly* (darbar).
Rajasthan, India, between 1865 and 1890. Print on albumen paper. 19 × 27.6 cm. Paris, Musée du Quai Branly
– Jacques Chirac, Inv. PP0020538

Cat. 23 Anonymous. *Rajput Prince*. Rajasthan, India, between 1860 and 1895. Aristotype print mounted on an album.
24.5 × 18.8 cm. Paris, Musée du Quai Branly – Jacques Chirac, Inv. PA000351.37

Cat. 24 Anonymous. *Young Woman on a Balcony*. Rajasthan, India, 1930–1950. Print on baryta paper.
29 × 23.7 cm. Paris, Musée du Quai Branly – Jacques Chirac, Inv. PP0205144

Cat. 25   Samuel Bourne (1834–1912). *Jag Mandir's Palace on Lake Pichhola, Udaipur*. Rajasthan, India, 1873.
Print on albumen paper. 18.5 cm × 31.5 cm. Paris, Musée National des Arts Asiatiques – Guimet, Inv. AP15344

Cat. 26* *Prince in his* zenana *(women's chambers)*. North India, Mughal school, c. 1740. Gouache, gold, and silver
on paper. 45 × 32 cm. Paris, Bibliothèque Nationale de France, Prints and Photography Department, Inv. Réserve Od 44.
Gift of Colonel Gentil, 1785.

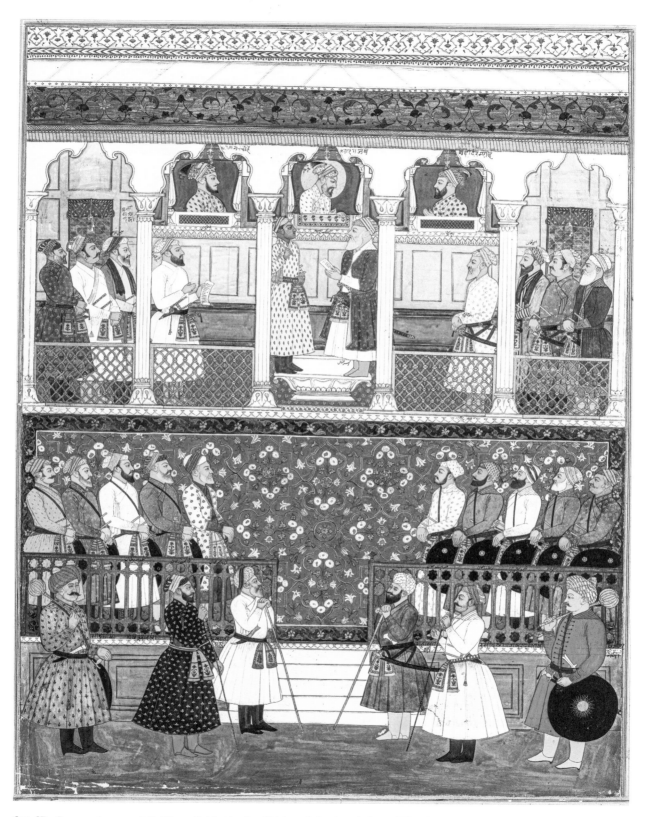

Cat. 27 *Emperor Aurangzeb Holding a Public Hearing*. Udaipur, Rajasthan, India, c. 1710–1720. Gouache on paper.
51 × 39 cm. Abu Dhabi, Louvre Abu Dhabi, LAD 2012.092

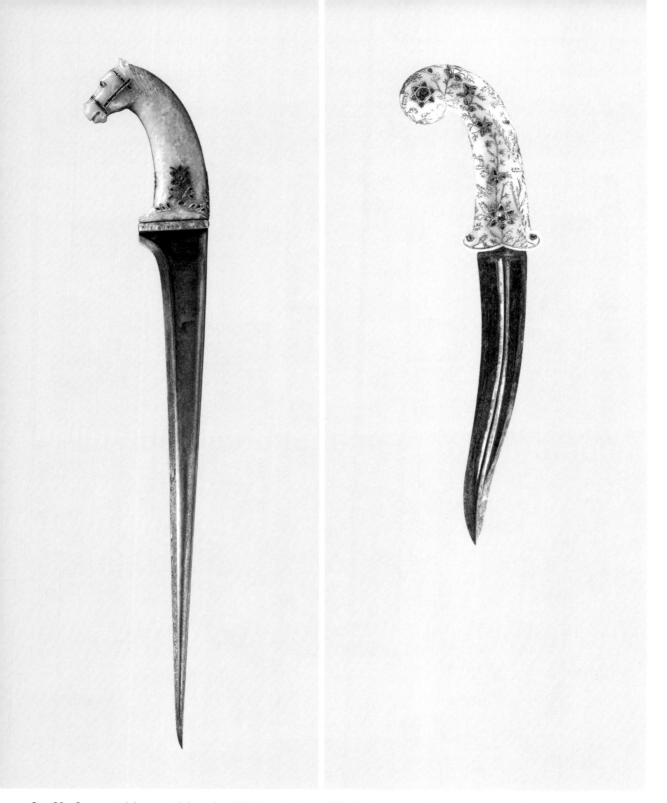

Cat. 28   Ceremonial dagger with horsehead hilt. North India, c. 1870. Steel, green nephrite, gemstones, gold.
55 × 10 cm. Abu Dhabi, Louvre Abu Dhabi, LAD 2014.014

Cat. 29   Ceremonial dagger with a volute-shaped hilt. India, 19th century. Jade inlaid with gold and precious
stones, steel. 32 × 9 × 2.5 cm. Abu Dhabi, Louvre Abu Dhabi, LAD 2014.012

Cat. 31   Spheroidal box. Mughal India, early 17th century. Rock crystal, silver, gold, rubies, emeralds.
Carved rock crystal and *Kundan* technique. H. 5.66 cm; D 5.14 cm. Kuwait, al-Sabah Collection, Inv. LNS 209 HS

Cat. 32   Hookah reservoir. Mughal India, 18th century. Jade, rubies, emeralds, gold. Carved jade with
the *Kundan* technique. 19.6 × 18 cm. Kuwait, al-Sabah Collection, Inv. LNS 635 HS

Found throughout the empire, jade and precious gemstones reflect the importance of the Mughal dynasty's
conquests and trade connections. The technique of inlaying these gemstones with exceptionally pure and
fine gold leaf (*Kundan*) produced objects of exquisite luxury.

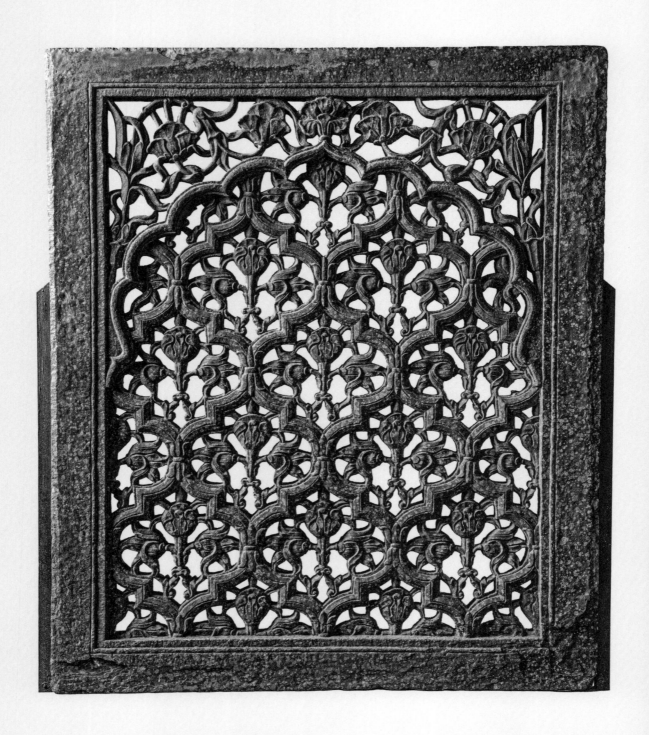

Cat. 33   Openwork architectural panel (*jali*). Agra region, Mughal India, c. 1630–1650.
Red sandstone. 125 × 105 × 75 cm. Abu Dhabi, Louvre Abu Dhabi, LAD 2020.109.002

Cat. 34   Openwork architectural panel (*jali*). Agra region, Mughal India, c. 1630–1650.
Red sandstone. 125 × 105 × 75 cm. Abu Dhabi, Louvre Abu Dhabi, LAD 2020.109.001

'Ray's films follow the journey of their characters and describe the complexity of their relationships, their thirst for emancipation, and their questions.'

Satyajit Ray: An Alternative Way of Filming India

EVA MARKOVITS

An abandoned house, a motionless dog, a snake slithering among the stones. A cart pulled by two cows crosses the field and, in the background, three silent and melancholic faces – those of a young boy and his parents who contemplate the life they are about to leave – while a bamboo flute strikes the last notes of the film.

On board a ship returning from England in 1950, Satyajit Ray (1921–1992) wrapped up his first film treatment,[1] and a long-standing project: the adaptation of *Pather Panchali*, Bibhutibhushan Bandopadhyay's 1928 popular Bengali bildungsroman, both created after the revelation of Vittorio De Sica's *Bicycle Thieves* (1948), a masterpiece of Italian neorealism. The first part of the Apu Trilogy, *Song of the Little Road* (1955), is Ray's first film in a long and prolific oeuvre that spanned 37 films until Ray's death. When, after many setbacks, it was released, the Bengali audience had never seen such a film. Shot on location, it portrays the life, joys, and sorrows of the Roy family – Apu, Durga, and their parents – in a remote Bengali village. It is accompanied by a soundtrack, but there is no musical sequence, which was unheard of in Indian talkies. The film ends with the departure of the family to Benares, compelled by poverty and the impossibility of restoring their ancestral home. Highly acclaimed in Bengal, the film received very positive reviews abroad, particularly in France, where it was screened in Cannes, but above all, in England. Satyajit Ray's career was launched while the second part of the Apu trilogy,

1.
A long text that provides an outline of the film's plot and its main scenes.

2.
Our Films, Their Films, by Satyajit Ray, Mumbai, Orient Longman Limited, 1976, p. 22.

The Unvanquished (1956), which won the Golden Lion award at the 1957 Venice Film Festival, brought him to the forefront of the international scene.

IN SEARCH OF REALITY

Ray's filmography always followed a parallel path to mainstream cinema produced by the studios in Bombay (present-day Mumbai). Something that he did not hold dear to his heart, it was a cinema with a repetitive style and mise en scène, showing popular melodramas with their musical numbers that flourished in the 1940s and 1950s – later called Bollywood. The only filmmaker who found favour in his eyes was Guru Dutt, the director of *The Thirsty One* (1957), a lavish film respectful of conventions, but steeped in great poetry. While he had not yet become a filmmaker but was still running a film club, Satyajit Ray, a passionate cinephile, wrote a text in 1947 eloquently entitled: 'What is Wrong with Indian Films?' He writes: 'It should be realised that the average American film is a bad model, if only because it depicts a way of life so utterly at variance with our own. [...] What the Indian cinema needs today is not more gloss, but more imagination, more integrity, and a more intelligent appreciation of the limitations of the medium.'[2] However, this statement does not reflect a rejection of American cinema. On the contrary, Hollywood was his first school and Ray greatly admired Ernst Lubitsch, Billy Wilder, as well as Frank Capra and John Ford. Rather, he rejected its mass production, which was exported worldwide and, according to him, atrophied creativity. Saturated with Hollywood cinema, he sought, whenever he could, to fill his gaps and those of his peers with Soviet and European cinema. The discovery of Italian neorealism struck him. The frantic pursuit of the thief by Antonio Ricci and his son in *Bicycle Thieves*, a metaphor for the misery of post-war Italy, moved him deeply and echoed his own cinematic intuitions.[3] The elements that impressed him and encouraged him to follow this movement were the adoption of location shooting, the use of non-professional actors, and the modest budget that was more than sufficient to produce such a powerful film, as indicated by the final paragraph of his article on Italian neorealist films. He writes: '*Bicycle Thieves* is a triumphant rediscovery of the fundamentals of cinema, and De Sica has openly acknowledged his debt to Chaplin. The simple universality of its theme, the effectiveness of its treatment, and the low cost of its production make it an ideal film for the Indian filmmaker to study. [...] For a popular medium, the best kind of inspiration should derive from life and have its roots in it. No amount of technical polish can make up for the artificiality of themes and dishonesty of treatment. The Indian filmmaker must turn to life, to reality. De Sica, and *not* De Mille, should be his ideal.'[4] The way De Sica used Rome and its suburbs as a backdrop impressed him and is echoed in the way Ray filmed the village and the countryside in the *Song of the Little Road*'s main locations. They emphasise the sense of reality that he was aiming for, far from the artificiality of studio sets. Thus, it contrasted with the fantasised India portrayed by many popular films in the wake of the Hollywood dream factory. It is worth mentioning that before, in 1950, it was Jean Renoir's encouragement that Satyajit Ray received in Calcutta, during a location scout for *The River* (1951), in which he participated, motivating him to become a filmmaker. Ray admired the humanism and exploration of human relationships in the work of Renoir who was to become his mentor,

3.
He was not the only one in India to be deeply struck by this film: this was also the case for Bimal Roy, one of the few popular Bengali directors whom Ray respected, and whose film *Do Bigha Zamin* (1953) received the International Prize at the Cannes Film Festival in 1954. With its limited number of musical sequences and its realistic plot and style, it echoes *Bicycle Thieves*. While shooting his film, Ray saw Bimal Roy's film at a festival in Calcutta (present-day Kolkata) and was in no doubt as to the path he was following.

4.
Our Films, Their Films, by Satyajit Ray, op. cit., p. 127.

5.
This storyboard is kept at the Cinémathèque française in Paris and selected plates can be viewed online.

6.
Two years before him, Ritwik Ghatak, a major Bengali filmmaker often overshadowed by Ray, directed *The Citizen* (1952), which depicts a family struggling to survive in the aftermath of the Partition in Calcutta (following the departure of the British, the Partition of India in August 1947 led to the creation of two independent states, India and Pakistan, and to religious violence between Hindus and Muslims). This film was not shown until 25 years after it was shot.

7.
A raga is a precise melodic framework on which musicians improvise.

so much so that his influence can be seen in many of his films.

A VISUAL LYRICISM

Ray did not write a script for *Song of the Little Road*, but instead relied on his notes and storyboard [fig. 23].[5] While this process was unheard of in India and surely hindered him in his fruitless search for producers, it reveals a visual and graphic approach that is central to his films. After an extremely complicated filming (lack of financing, a one-year interruption) and five years of hard work, the film was finally completed. This immersion in rural India and its authenticity, which contrasts so strongly with mainstream commercial cinema, was quite daring.[6] The stamp of neorealism was immediately recognised by some critics. This classification is undeniable but its nuances should be explained further.

The poetry and lyricism typical of Ray's work, which give a musical rhythm to some of the sequences, are highly personal and are absent in the films of his Italian counterparts. The nearly silent sequence of the arrival of the monsoon in *Song of the Little Road* is a pure moment of contemplation [cat. 35]. Like a ballet, dragonflies, lotus flowers, and water lilies move to the rhythm of the music by the great Indian composer, Ravi Shankar, who performs the rain raga[7] on the sitar. This improvisation resonates with a parallel montage, which alternates between nature awakening, the sound of the storm, Apu and Durga delighting in the liberating but violent rain, and their mother worrying about their absence. This scene is emblematic of what Ray describes in a letter that he sent from London to Bansi Chandragupta, his faithful art director: 'The entire conventional approach (as exemplified by even the best American and British films) is wrong. Because the conventional approach tells you that the best way to tell a story is to leave out all except those elements which are directly related to the story, while the

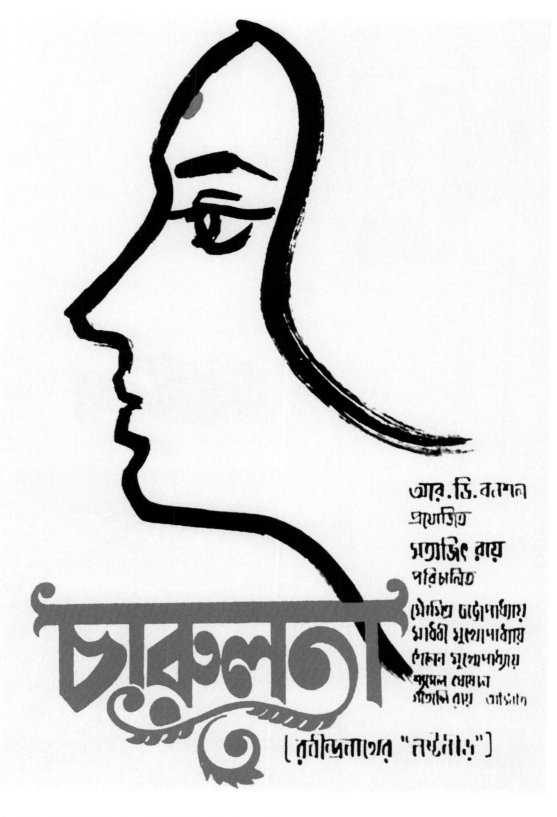

Fig. 19   Poster for *The Lonely Wife* (*Charulata*, 1964), designed by Satyajit Ray. © RDB Entertainments, India

Fig. 20   Benode Behari Mukherjee (1904–1980). *Untitled (Santhals)*. Watercolour on paper.
32 × 56 cm. New Delhi, DAG

Fig. 21   Cover of the 20th anniversary special issue of the children's magazine *Sandesh*, 1982,
drawing by Satyajit Ray. 24.5 x 19 cm. Kolkata, Society for the Preservation of Satyajit Ray Archives

master's work clearly indicates that if your theme is strong and simple, then you can include a hundred little, apparently, irrelevant details which, instead of obscuring the theme, only help to intensify it by contrast, and in addition, create the illusion of actuality better'.[8] The monsoon sequence is based on this principle of contrasts. While it is necessary to the plot (the torrential downpour causes Durga's fatal illness), it is also full of fascinating visual details bursting with life. It is precisely this attention to life through its everyday aspects, rather than the spectacle, that fundamentally distinguishes Ray from his contemporary Bombay counterparts. When film studios portray poverty, they do so by glorifying it. Mehboob Khan's *Mother India* (1957), which tells the story of a young peasant struggling to survive after her husband abandoned her and her children, was a blockbuster. As a metaphor for the Indian nation, she is the quintessential heroine of an epic and spectacular story, disconnected from reality. In Ray's films, understatement prevails, but silence speaks volumes.

A MULTIFACETED ARTIST

Understanding that this eye for nature and bodies, and more broadly, the pictorial nature of Ray's work, is a family trait passed down from father to son, is crucial. Both his grandfather and father were multifaceted artists: his grandfather, Upendrakishore Ray, was a printer, writer, illustrator, musician, and composer, while his father, Sukumar Ray, was a poet, writer, and illustrator. Although he never knew them – his father died when he was two years old – Satyajit Ray also had more than one string to his bow: he was a draughtsman, illustrator, graphic designer, writer, composer, as well as a filmmaker. In the early 1940s, he studied drawing and painting in Santiniketan, at the art school and university established by Artist and Writer Rabindranath Tagore, a prominent Bengali figure, close to the Ray family, and recipient of the 1913 Nobel Prize in Literature. Ray was already quite familiar with Western painting, but in this school he discovered several Indian pictorial movements that greatly influenced him. Among them was the Bengal School (1910s–1920s, **fig. 20**), which sought to develop a contemporary Indian style,

8.
Excerpt from Satyajit Ray's letter to Bansi Chandragupta quoted by Andrew Robinson in *Satyajit Ray: The Inner Eye*, Berkeley, University of California Press, 1989, p. 72.

9.
A wealthy landowner.

10.
'Silence on tourne' (1965) in *Écrits sur le cinéma, Satyajit Ray*, Éditions Jean-Claude Lattès, Paris, 1982, p. 56.

born in reaction against the Western academic painting taught in India at the time, and which advocated for a revival of Indian visual traditions. There, he learned the importance of details that express something bigger, a concept that was to become an essential element of his mise en scène, full of visual metaphors and eloquent close-ups. In the end, he did not have the makings of a painter, so he left Santiniketan and in order to make a living as a newlywed, he became a graphic designer for an advertising agency in Calcutta, DJ Keymer, and was an illustrator for publishing houses. The experience of working with graphic elements before becoming a filmmaker, later nourished Satyajit Ray's films and cinematic language, as well as his sets, costumes, and posters.

A UNIVERSAL FILMMAKER

Ray's filmography is extremely versatile, with a rich variety of social backgrounds, sets, and cinematic forms. The downfall of a *zamindar*[9] in *The Music Room* (1959), the intellectual emancipation of a young woman in late 19th-century Bengal in *The Lonely Wife (Charulata)* (1964, **fig. 19**), the haunted forest of *The Adventures of Goopy and Bagha* (1969), a young man seeking work in contemporary Calcutta of the 1970s in *The Adversary* (1971), the fate of the victims of the Bengal famine of 1943 in *Distant Thunder* (1973), or documentaries portraying prominent artists (Tagore, his father, the painter Benode Behari Mukherjee) are all stories and contexts that depict an era and its turmoil without disorienting an audience unfamiliar with India – or more specifically, Bengal, since he mainly explored that region. All these films follow the journey of their characters and describe the complexity of their relationships, their thirst for emancipation, and their questions. This universality distinguishes him from other contemporary filmmakers such as Ritwik Ghatak or Mrinal Sen whose scripts, that could be quite political, are rooted in the traumas of India's independence in 1947 and the secession of Pakistan. Ray was determined to reach a wide audience because he believed that cinema was 'the noblest of the commercial arts'.[10] This is why, in 1961, he relaunched the *Sandesh* magazine [**fig. 21**] created by his grandfather, for which he wrote hundreds of illustrated short stories for children, featuring the recurring characters of Feluda and Professor Shonku, which he also adapted to film. Ray's reputation for his film work is greater internationally than in his own country where his films did not circulate much outside the borders of Bengal due to subtitling issues with India's several official languages. This fame has earned him criticism since it was perceived as an interest to pursue an international audience, instead of remaining India-centric; a misunderstanding of his dedication to his heritage that characterised his work. An heir to the Bengali Renaissance, a cultural movement that surfaced at the end of the 19th century among the cosmopolitan and liberal Bengali elite (rejection of the caste system, the emancipation of women) that advocated for independence but had a complex relationship with colonisation and England, Satyajit Ray was a 'rare mix of East and West', to quote his own words about his ancestors. This mixture naturally permeates his films, which certainly explains the international appeal of his work.

11.
Ekti Shishir Bindu, Rabindranath Tagore, quoted by Satyajit Ray, in Folke Isaksson, 'The Dewdrop on a Blade of Grass: Satyajit Ray in Conversation', *Sight and Sound*, Summer 1970.

POSTERITY

As a leading exponent of auteur cinema, Ray, along with other directors, has inspired generations of filmmakers. He has strongly influenced those who were part of the 'Parallel Cinema' movement, which emerged in the late 1960s in various parts of India and whose major figures were Kumar Shahani, John Abraham, and Aparna Sen (many of whom were students of Ghatak's at the Film and Television Institute in Pune, the country's leading film school). As its name suggests, this movement followed a different path from Bollywood; influenced by the European new waves, aesthetics, and a certain left-wing ideology that permeated Bengali cinema, this radical cinema undoubtedly found its inspiration in *Song of the Little Road*, a seminal film in many ways. Watching Ray's films is like watching the reflection of a multi-sided, complex, and prolific India, a mirror of the world which resonates with the poem Tagore wrote for the young Ray when he visited him, and which would be his guiding light: 'I travelled miles for many a year/ I spent a lot in lands afar/ I've gone to see mountains, the oceans I've been to view/ But I haven't seen with these eyes/ Just two steps from my home lies/ On a sheaf of (paddy) grain, a glistening drop of dew/ A drop which reflects in its convexity the whole universe around it'.[11]

Fig. 22   Satyajit Ray on the filming of *The Golden Fortress* in 1974

Fig. 23   Still from Satyajit Ray's storyboard for *Song of the Little Road* (1955). Paris, Cinémathèque française

Cat. 35   Stills from the monsoon sequence in *Song of the Little Road* (1955), directed by Satyajit Ray

Nayanthara in *Nose-ring Goddess* (2020), directed by R J Balaji and N J Saravanan (see fig. 29, page 125)

Aesthetic and Commercial Circulation

'In cinema, the use of Tamil generates a symbolic, embodied and affective connection to 'Tamilness' and Tamil identity. Movie dialogues and songs often glorify and celebrate [...] the Tamil language, people, culture, and identity.'

Tamil Cinema: Cult of Actors and Star System

SELVARAJ VELAYUTHAM

Cinema pervades Indian society with its social imaginary and incarnations in both particular and peculiar ways according to its local origins. India is one of the largest producers of films in the world and the cinemas of India are as culturally and linguistically diverse as the nation-state. Yet, for many, Bollywood, the popular name given to the Bombay (present-day Mumbai) based Hindi film industry, is Indian cinema *par excellence*. The idea of Indian cinema is profoundly determined and reproduced through the lens of Bollywood owing to its huge commercial success both in India and elsewhere. The cultural hegemony and dominance of Bollywood within the Indian film industry has cast a long shadow over the rich complexities and ethnolinguistic specific cinematic traditions of India that include Bengali, Urdu, Marathi, Gujarati, Assamese, Malayalam, Kannada, Telugu, and Tamil language film industries, often referred to as 'regional cinema' which are equally prolific and popular in their own right. A close reading of the various Indian language films will reveal that many differences and nuances exist between them. They not only differ in their use of language (including regional variations), specific historical and cultural references, regional themes and styles but also in the ways in which they relate to their diasporic audience and in their global circulation.

Since its inception in the second decade of the 20th century, Tamil cinema has grown into a multimillion-dollar industry. Located in the Chennai district of Kodambakkam, Tamil Nadu's cinema city, it is one of the powerhouses of Indian cinema. Sometimes referred to as

1.
Yves Thoraval,
The Cinemas of India,
Macmillan India
Limited, New Delhi,
2000, p. 35.

Kollywood, an amalgam of the words Kodambakkam and Hollywood, Tamil cinema has a long history comparable to the other Indian language cinemas. As Yves Thoraval[1] observes, the end of the silent era also marked the birth of a new entity, 'South Indian cinema' – embracing Tamil, Telugu, Kannada, and Malayalam cinema – with Madras (present-day Chennai)) as the centre of production. The South Indian Telugu and Tamil language cinemas collectively produce more than eight hundred films annually as compared to Bollywood. According to the Central Board of Film Certification a total of 501 Hindi, 463 Telugu, and 423 Tamil language feature-length films were certified in 2021. Tamil cinema's audience is primarily Tamil-speaking and spread across India or globally in the diaspora. Its overseas audiences are in Sri Lanka, Malaysia, Singapore, Mauritius, South Africa, the Middle East, Europe, North America, Australia, and New Zealand, where both older and recent Tamil migrants reside.

ETHNO-LINGUISTIC DISTINCTIVENESS OF TAMIL CINEMA

Tamil cinema has a number of distinct characteristics that are unique to this industry. First, it has to be said that language is a critical marker of distinction. Though Tamil is recognized as one of India's national languages it is not a *lingua franca*. The Tamil language is only widely spoken in the state of Tamil Nadu. It is a classical living language and belongs to the Dravidian language

Fig. 24   M G Ramachandran and J Jayalalitha in *Protector* (1967), directed by P Neelakantan

Fig. 25   M G Ramachandran in *Protector* (1967), directed by P Neelakantan

group. The ancient origin, roots, and literary tradition of the Tamil language have given impetus to the production of a powerful myth and trope of signification between language, identity, territory, and 'Tamilness'. It is a language imbued with tradition and ethnonationalism. As the Historian Sumathi Ramaswamy[2] writes in her enthralling book, *Language Devotion in Tamil India*, for the Tamils 'the state of the language mirrors the state of its speakers; language is the essence of their culture, the bearer of their traditions, and the vehicle of their thoughts from time immemorial.' Such profound overtures and self-proclamations are not only found in the political culture of Tamil Nadu but also in Tamil cinema.

In cinema, the use of Tamil generates a symbolic, embodied and affective connection to 'Tamilness' and Tamil identity. Movie dialogues and songs often glorify and celebrate (often non-diegetically) the Tamil language, people, culture, and identity. This locates both the film and the audience within a particular ethnonational imaginary and linguistic space which is Tamil and Tamil only.[3] For instance, frequent articulation of Tamil Nadu (Tamil country) or Tamilakam ('*akam*' means home or interior) which refers to the land of Tamil language, culture, and/or people, is a powerful signifier. As Jacob Pandian[4] points out, it evokes the imagery of an internal psychic/emotional unity of all Tamils against the 'external other'. An important point to stress here is that because of the specificities of the language, Tamil cinema always portrays the Tamils while Hindi cinema, more often than not, represents an 'Indian' without an ethno-specific identity. The characters of Bollywood cinema are supposedly pan-Indian. Moreover, Tamil cinema is set in particular locations in Tamil Nadu that usually employ the respective district's inflections or Tamil dialects such as the Madras Bashai of Chennai, Kongu dialect of Coimbatore, Thanjavur, Tirunelveli, Ramanathapuram, and so forth.

CULT HEROES OF TAMIL SCREENS AND BEYOND

The year 1916 is often marked as the birth of Tamil cinema with the establishment of the first studio in Madras, the India Film Company, and

2.
Sumathi Ramaswamy, *Passions of the Tongue. Language Devotion in Tamil India, 1891–1970*. University of California Press, Berkeley, Los Angeles, London, 1997, p. 244.

3.
Selvaraj Velayutham (ed), *Tamil Cinema: The Cultural Politics of India's Other Tamil Cinema*, Routledge, London, 2008.

4.
Jacob Pandian, *The Making of India and Indian Traditions*, Prentice Hall, New Jersey, 1995.

the release of the first South Indian feature-length film, *The Destruction of Keechakan*, produced and directed by R Nataraja Mudaliar. Most of the films in the silent period were mythological stories drawn from religious epics and folklores. The first Tamil talkie released in 1931 was *Kalidas* directed by H M Reddy, based on the legendary Sanskrit poet. As soon as the talkies arrived, the Tamil film industry began to develop rapidly, ushering into cinema's history a long list of successful and immensely popular actors, producers, directors, scriptwriters, music composers, and singers. Media moguls such as S S Vasan, A V Meyyappan (AVM) and T R Sundaram, to name just a few, established film studios, production companies and cinema halls giving impetus to the growth of the industry. During the pre-war period, films embraced new genres in addition to mythological ones. Ellis Duncan's *Two Sisters* (1936), and K Subrahmanyam's *Girl Saint* (1937) adopted contemporary social themes such as family disputes and caste discrimination. Other films like H M Reddy's *Mathurabhoomi* (1939) and K Subrahmanya's *Land of Sacrifice* (1939) featured strong overtones of anti-British sentiments, Indian nationalism, and glorified the ideals of Mahatma Gandhi.

The founding of the Dravida Munnetra Kazhagam (DMK) in 1949 by C N Annadurai, a film writer, who was joined by M Karunanidhi, another film writer, and a number of film actors, including N S Krishnan, K R Ramasway, S S Rajendran, Shivaji Ganesan, and M G Ramachandran (MGR, **fig. 24 and fig. 25**) mobilised an entire generation of Tamil cinema audience members around the Dravidian movement. Annadurai's screenplays *Good Brother* (1948), *Servant Maid* (1949) and M Karunanidhi's *The Goddess* (1952), not only attacked the upper caste/classes, Brahmanism, and hypocrisy of religion, but also championed high literary Tamil and Tamil cultural identity. The rise of Dravidian politics, both in the political landscape as well as on Tamil film screens, came to fruition with the defeat of the Indian National Congress in the general elections of 1967. The demise of Congress's twenty-year reign in Tamil Nadu also marked the beginning of state-based party politics in Tamil Nadu and beyond. The political tussle between M Karunanidhi and M G Ramachandran, following the death of Annadurai in 1969, resulted in the latter forming the All India Anna Dravida Munnetra Kazhagam (AIADMK). The post-war period also saw the proliferation of Tamil movies that were, on the one hand, infused and influenced by Dravidian politics and, on the other hand, had more melodramas and social themes. The key features of the period include major stars such as Gemini Ganesan, Savitri, Bhanumathi, Saroja Devi, and Jayalalitha [fig. 24]; and film narratives highlighting and driven by moral imperatives associated with social ills, family breakdowns, good versus bad, overcoming of social difficulties, and subaltern struggles.

Between the 1970s and the 1990s, Tamil cinema was reinvigorated by the arrival of new and young talents as the stars of earlier decades faded away or entered retirement. These three decades saw the entry of the second generation of actors like Kamal Haasan [fig. 26], Rajinikanth [fig. 30 to fig. 34], Vijayakanth, Saritha, and Sridevi in lead roles. This period witnessed the emergence of neo-nativity films – a term coined by Sundar Kaali[5] – referring to a genre that was preoccupied with a return to the rural roots of Tamil culture, an aggrandisement of tradition and the sensory ambience of the Tamil countryside. Directors like Bharathiraja, Bhagyaraj, Balu Mahendra, and T Rajender were emblematic of neo-nativity Tamil cinema and principally devoted themselves to elevating the rural experience, as quintessentially rooted in Tamil identity and culture. They presented a powerful counter-narrative to rapid urbanisation and dilution of

5.
Sundar Kaali, 'Narrating Seduction: Vicissitudes of the sexed subject in Tamil nativity film', In *Making Meaning in Indian Cinema*, edited by Ravi S Vasudevan, Oxford University Press, New Delhi, 2000, p. 168–90.

Tamil identity taking place in urban centres in Tamil Nadu. By the 1990s, with the opening of India's economy, popular Indian cinema began to reach out to its global diasporic audience. Tamil cinema also responded by way of Director Mani Ratnam. His trilogy *Rose* (1992), *Bombay* (1995), and *From the Heart* (1998), explores communal violence, separatism, Indian patriotism, and the resilience of the Indian state.

In the footsteps of M G Ramachandran and Jayalalitha who used cinema as a platform to launch their political careers, other film stars like Vijayakanth, Varalaxmi Sarathkumar [fig. 28], and Kamal Hassan have made headway in Tamil Nadu politics. By the turn of the century, Tamil cinema would usher in a new wave of young stars who have become immensely popular, including actors such as Ajith, Vijay [fig. 27], Dhanush, Jayam Ravi, Suriya, Sivakarthikeyan, Vijay Sethupathi, Silambarasan, Trisha, and Nayanthara [fig. 29]. A notable feature of the cult of actors and star system within Tamil cinema is the work of fan clubs. There are thousands of fan club associations throughout Tamil Nadu that revere yesteryear stars like Sivaji Ganesan and MGR; superstars like Rajnikanth; and present-day heroes like Ajith and Vijay. These community organisations, which mostly support male actors and with members who are typically young men, have had a major influence in creating mass followings and cult statuses around individual actors, making Tamil cinema a truly interesting and unique form of popular culture.

Fig. 26   Kamal Haasan in his own film *Virumandi* (2004)

Fig. 27   Vijay in *Sarkar* (*Government*, 2018), directed by A R Murugadoss

Fig. 28   Varalaxmi Sarathkumar in *Danny* (2020), directed by Santhanamoorthy

'Rajinikanth challenged the status quo not only by his role as an antagonist but by his very presence. He was Tamil cinema's own subversive star who caught everyone's attention.'

Rajinikanth: The Superstar from the Global South

SWARNAVEL ESWARAN

Rajinikanth (born as Shivaji Rao Gaekwad on 12 December 1950) in Bangalore, South India, is still a highly sought-after star after an illustrious career of 47 years as an exceedingly popular actor in Tamil cinema, one of the largest and oldest cinema industries in the world. Over the last five decades, his eventful career is without parallel as far as sustained box office success and popularity are concerned, starting with his debut in *Rare Melodies* (1975) directed by his mentor K Balachander. In India, 1975 was a tumultuous year under the Emergency act when democratic rights were suspended; many leaders of the opposition were arrested and imprisoned; and fundamental rights were suppressed, including freedom of speech, particularly when it criticised the state. Against this backdrop, an unusual villain with his kinetic style of body movements and gestures garnered attention.

Rajinikanth was different from the older generation of actors like MGR or the famous villains such as Nambiar, mainly because of his 'man from the neighbourhood' appearance. From his first film onward, he stood out because of his presence, gestures like throwing a cigarette out of his pants pocket and effortlessly catching it, or playing around with his eyeglasses with both hands. Regardless of his roles, his noticeable style captured the audience's attention. It was a statement, not only regarding his youthful energy but also about acknowledging his presence. More importantly, it was an assertion of self-respect and dignity. Rajinikanth was the first dark-skinned villain/hero, who was not just a villain's henchman. In contrast to 'the angry young man' from the north, Amitabh Bachchan, Rajinikanth challenged the status quo not only

by his role as an antagonist but by his very presence. He was Tamil cinema's own subversive star who caught everyone's attention.

Rajinikanth's charm brought in audiences. Until 1977, he acted in the roles of the antagonist in successful films, like *Three Knots*, (1976) by K Balachander, which had his rival Kamal Haasan and Sridevi playing the protagonists. Director Bharathiraja launched his career with the same trio in *At Age 16* (1977). These films helped showcase Rajinikanth's range as an actor from a city-bred man to a rustic character. The critical acclaim, along with the box office appeal, led to him being cast as the hero with a good heart who would support and marry the victim of his womanising friend in *Bhuvana Is a Mystery* (1977). It was directed by S P Muthuraman, who would work with Rajinikanth over the next two decades. They collaborated on 25 films, including the highly successful *Raging Bull* (1980) and *The Third Eye* (1981), which paved the way for Rajinikanth's continued success in the 1980s. In this crucial decade, he was the most prolific, acting in films by all the top mainstream directors, including his mentor Balachander, and production houses like AVM Studios. His action-hero image appealed to the audiences in the urban and rural spaces, and his penchant for comedy could draw in family audiences.

Films like *Thorn and Flower* (1978) by Mahendran [fig. 31], an iconic film of the postclassical Tamil cinema, which moved increasingly away from the studio indoors, and *From Six to Sixty* (1979), one of his early films with Director S P Muthuraman, were critically acclaimed for his performances. Rajinikanth portrayed an older brother in both of these films. In the former, he played a ruffian with a mellow heart who would ultimately surrender his ego and allow his sister to marry his rival. While in the latter, he was an ordinary worker in a press who cares for his siblings and philosophically accepts the vicissitudes of life, leading to his success as a writer. Though such modest-budgeted films disappeared with his exponential rise as a preeminent star in the 1980s, they marked Rajinikanth as an action star who was the entire family's favourite, not just the male members. Therefore, the narratives of his films often had the subtext of the older brother who is willing to sacrifice for his family.

Juxtaposing the interior of the home with the increasingly global public sphere in the 1990s, the post-Gorbachev era saw Rajinikanth engaging extensively with community issues and later, in the new millennium, international issues like global warming and the environment. As India changed gears from Nehruvian socialism to liberalisation and privatisation of the West, Rajinikanth played superhero roles where it was not just the home but the entire community or region, maybe even the world at stake. The most iconic film in his career of 166 films, thus far, is *Baasha* (1995) by Suresh Krissna [fig. 32], wherein he plays the autorickshaw driver confronted with his past as a gangster in Bombay (present-day Mumbai). For the sake of his younger sister and brother, he takes on the powerful mafia, with the help of his community of drivers. *Baasha*'s colossal success across the borders opened the doors for the theatrical release of Rajinikanth's films in the UK, USA, and Australia, apart from the traditional market in the Tamil diaspora in Malaysia, Singapore, the Middle East, Sri Lanka, among other places. The last two decades, with the advent of digital cinema, have seen Rajinikanth's rise as a national Indian star who has a global market, particularly with the success of multimillion-dollar films like *Sivaji* (2007), *Robot* (2010, fig. 33), and *2.0* (2018, fig. 34), all of them directed by S Shankar – Tamil cinema's most expensive director, known for his extravagance. Having won all the major awards, including the Dadasaheb Phalke Award in 2019, the highest honour for the filmmaking fraternity in India, one could say that the undying idolisation of his fans who revere him like a demi-god, the enormous banners and cutouts at the theatres, and rituals like offerings of milk and sweets on the release of his films, keep him going at the age of 71.

Fig. 30   Rajinikanth in *They* (1977), directed by K Balachander

Fig. 32　Rajinikanth in *Baasha* (1995), directed by Suresh Krishna

Fig. 33   Rajinikanth and Aishwarya Rai in *Robot* (2010), directed by S Shankar

Fig. 34 Rajinikanth in *2.0* (2018), directed by S Shankar

135

'Sometimes sought after, and sometimes fought against, Indian films in Egypt illustrate the intimate links between the film industry, national politics, and foreign affairs.'

From Bombay to Cairo, Peace and War(s) for Hindi Films

NÉMÉSIS SROUR

'Forget Hollywood, Egyptians Are in Love with Bollywood', headlined the website of a US-based radio station on 17 May 2015.[1] The idea that Arabs are fond of Indian films is nothing new and has been around for several decades. In 1965, the French Cinema Historian Georges Sadoul had already pointed out the cultural affinities between Indian films and the Arab filmgoers: 'Regarding the importance of Indian cinema in Arab countries, it is a kind of innate spontaneity that I cannot explain.'[2] Indeed, in the 1960s, Indian films circulated in several countries of the Arab world such as Egypt, Iraq, Lebanon, and Syria. Additionally, the films' great popularity among French and European critics might be explained by their sheer astonishment for a trend in cinema they didn't understand. But, other than a popular trend, what is it really all about? In fact, Indian films in Egypt have had a stormy history. Sometimes sought after, and sometimes fought against, Indian films in Egypt illustrate the intimate links between the film industry, national politics, and foreign affairs.

1.
Laura Dean, 'Forget Hollywood, Egyptians Are in Love with Bollywood', *Public Radio International*, 17 May 2015, https://www.pri.org/stories/2015-05-17/forget-hollywood-egyptians-are-love-bollywood.

2.
Centre interarabe du cinéma et de la télévision, "Cinéma et cultures arabes. IVe conférence de la table ronde organisée avec l'aide technique de l'Unesco", Beirut, 25 October 1965.

3.
'Une belle manifestation d'amitié indo-égyptienne', *Le Progrès égyptien*, 17 March 1953, p. 3.

4.
Richard Edmund Ward, *India's pro-Arab Policy: A Study in Continuity*, Praeger, New York/Westport/London, 1992.

5.
Le Progrès égyptien, op. cit.

1954: THE NASSER-NEHRU AGREEMENT, CINEMA AS A POLITICAL TOOL FOR THE 'ART OF PEACE'[3]

On 4 January 1954, Egypt saw its first 'Hindu' film, as it then was called. In Egypt, the screening of Indian films occurred at a time of political rapprochement between the future Egyptian President, Nasser, and the Indian Prime Minister, Nehru, as part of the non-aligned movement. Bringing the Middle East back to the heart of Indian foreign policy, it first appeared to be 'Cairo-centric',[4] even more than pro-Arab. In addition to a trade agreement signed in May 1953, the cultural relationship between the two countries was formalised earlier in March 1953 by the creation of the India-Egypt Association, which aimed to strengthen 'the fraternity between two great nations' by means of the exchange of literary works, films, and the organisation of cultural events.[5] The idea of putting film at the service of foreign policy is consistent with the discourse of the Bombay (present-day Mumbai) film industry. In 1955, a film distributor explained: 'Indian films enjoy increasing popularity in the Far East and Middle East countries. [...] But I believe that if both Government and the Industry set themselves fully to the task of expanding the foreign market, it will not only help the Industry but also help to foster friendly international relations for us.'[6]

How can we explain the ways in which cinema was advocated for as a political tool by the industry players? At the time, apart from its patriotic or pedagogical purposes, the cinematographic medium was deeply despised by the Indian ruling elites. Promoting the political interest of cinema, particularly in international diplomacy, appeared to be a strategic argument to gain access to the international market, which was then subjected to strict government regulations.

In 1954, benefiting from a supportive and amenable environment, Indian films began to form part of the cinematographic landscape of Egypt's major cities. *Aan* (1952)[7] by Mehboob Khan, was released at the Strand cinema in Alexandria on 4 January 1954, and at the Miami cinema in Cairo [fig. 35], almost two years after its release in India. This film was the first Indian feature-length film to be produced in Technicolor and holds an exceptional place in the history of Indian cinema as it had an unprecedented international distribution.[8] The gala opening night of *Aan*, which took place under the patronage of the Liberation Committee directed by Nasser, demonstrates the very special atmosphere of the time, when culture and politics were purposely intertwined. The film's premiere was attended by members of the Revolutionary Council and by the Indian ambassador in Cairo. Attesting to the political dimension of this screening, the proceeds went to the Liberation Committee's health fund. The debut of this Hindi film, the first of its kind in 1950s Egypt, positioned it in a prestigious ecosystem, especially since it was screened in first-class cinemas[9]. While it was supported by the Egyptian government at the time, the Egyptian authorities in the 1970s became concerned about the growing presence of Asian films in the country.

6.
S K Patil, 'The Year in Retrospect. An Annual Survey of the Film Industry by Leading Spokesmen', *Filmfare*, 16 mars 1956, p. 6.

7.
The film was released in the United Kingdom and in the United States as *The Savage Princess*.

8.
Gayatri Chatterjee, *Mother India*, BFI Film Classics, London, British Film Institute, 2002.

9.
Cinemas in Egypt, whether first, second, or third class, were organised according to a ranking system whose main criterion was the price of the ticket. This material criterion was based on the location of the cinema and its programme. First category cinemas were located in central Cairo and mainly screened Hollywood, French, or Italian films.

10.
Kerry Segrave, *American Films Abroad: Hollywood's Domination of the World's Movie Screens from the 1890s to the Present*, McFarland, Jefferson/London, 1997.

11.
Tourya Guaaybess, *Télévisions arabes sur orbite : un système médiatique en mutation (1960-2004)*, Paris, CNRS éditions, 2013.

THE SIX-DAY WAR: AN 'INVASION' OF HINDI FILMS?

The idea of a cultural 'invasion' by cinema has surfaced at different times in political rhetoric, whether with American films in Egypt, Egyptian films in other Arab countries, or Indian films in Syria or Egypt. The Egyptian government's first wave of concern about Hindi films flourishing in their country emerged after the Six-Day War in 1967, which pitted Israel against Egypt, Jordan, and Syria. Its immediate consequence was an embargo on Western cultural products in Egypt. Not only was the number of English-language programmes on television reduced, but the third channel, which used to broadcast them, was closed. This war with Israel served as a pretext for political powers, that had long been displeased with the themes and values of American films, to officially ban them. The films were criticised for their portrayal of sex and violence, as well as the glamorising of wealth and luxury in a consumerist society. In the words of a theatre manager, 'Stopping American films would really have started a riot. But with the war and the downgrading of the United States' status in the public mind, the censor[s] had gained the upper hand.'[10] Instead, the Egyptian state decided to strengthen its diplomatic ties with the Soviet Union among others, which resulted in a significant increase in Soviet-produced programmes which were broadcasted on Egyptian television.[11] This conflictual political situation seemed to benefit Indian cinema, as stated in an article in *Film Trade*, the Indian cinema business magazine: 'West Asia has become a significant export market for Indian films after the beginning of hostilities between the Arabs and Israel. The Indian government's support for the Arab cause proves to be a blessing for the film industry. Even before the Arab-Israeli conflict, Indian films were gaining ground in this region. But American and British films were banned after the war, and this turned out to be a blessing in disguise that helped our

Fig. 35 Cinema Miami in the 1950s, Cairo

films gain a strong foothold in the region. The Ministry of Communications and Information Technology has been approached by some of the West Asian countries to supply them with two hundred Indian films. The ministry, in turn, tries to send as many as possible.'[12]

The popularity of Indian films grew as audiences in Cairo's cinemas changed in the late 1960s. Director Yousri Nasrallah explains: 'With the great catastrophe of 1967 and the destruction of the cities around Suez, an exodus to Cairo followed, which led to a change in the audience. The great American films had disappeared and in their place, from 1968–1969, we had karate films and Indian films instead. The atmosphere in cinemas was slowly changing, because the films targeted a much more populist audience, and families no longer attended. Macho comments became commonplace and there were even fights. This decline affected almost all cinemas: the Rivoli, the Radio and even the Kasr el-Nil, which had shifted from a *United Artists* programme to "karate films". Perhaps only the Metro was spared... Cinema in Cairo had become a man's business due to the population explosion and to changes in film supply.'[13] This populist male audience, now predominant in Cairo cinemas, recognised itself in the Hindi films of the time, thanks to emblematic roles such as Amitabh Bachchan, who embodied the character of 'the angry young man'.

From the 1970s onwards, a distinct shift took place: not only were there an unprecedented number of Hindi films, but there was also an almost continuous year-round programming, with a choice of roughly two different Hindi films per week. This was an unprecedented configuration. The growing popularity of Hindi films in Egypt coincided with the audience change, and the government sought to curb the popular trend very quickly. This is the paradox of Indian cinema's golden age: it did not occur during a favourable political context but emerged when legislation opposed it the most. How does this explain the reversal, and the constancy – at least for a while – of the popularity of these films?

12.
Film Trade,
26 July 1975.

13.
Marie-Claude Bénard,
*La Sortie au cinéma :
palaces et ciné-jardins
d'Égypte (1930-1980)*,
Marseille, Éditions
Parenthèses MMSH,
2016. The expression
'karate films', used
by Egyptian legislators,
refers to Hong Kong
cinema.

14.
These two holidays are
the most important
ones in the Muslim
calendar: al-Fitr
marks the breaking
of the fast at the
end of the month
of Ramadan, while
al-Adha celebrates
Abraham's submission
to God.

15.
The decree of the
Ministry of Culture
and Information dated
2 May 1974 goes
a step further, and
prohibits the import
or screening of karate
films, samurai films,
or any other similar
films nationwide.
See: Gehan Rachty
and Khalil Sabat
(ed.), *Importation
of Films for Cinema
and Television in Egypt:
A Study*, Unesco,
Paris, 1981,
p. 23.

1973: DOWN WITH 'KARATE FILMS', DOWN WITH INDIAN FILMS!

The legislative campaign against Hindi films in Egypt should be considered in the broader context of the policy aimed at protecting Egyptian filmmaking. This protectionism enabled the Egyptian industry to secure its place on the screens of its country, and to resist the threat of an international hegemony, whether it be Hollywood, French, Italian, or Indian cinema. In the 1970s, the volume of Indian films distributed in Egypt was subject to government import regulations for foreign films, and was limited to three hundred films per year. However, the Asian film category, which included Hong Kong films, was more strictly regulated than other foreign films, as their presence was limited to only five copies per year.

In 1973–1974, government decrees followed one after another with the same general purpose: to protect Egyptian films and their presence in cinemas as much as possible. A number of policies forced the presence of local films on screens: as long as an Egyptian film generated a minimum amount of revenue, it was forbidden for the cinema to stop showing it; all Egyptian cinemas had to screen local films on the occasion of the two major Muslim holidays, Eid al-Adha and Eid al-Fitr;[14] and Egyptian films were always to be given priority. In order to do this, the presence of Indian and 'karate films' had to be controlled and limited as much as possible. The decree of 10 March 1973, for example, prohibited the simultaneous screening of more than one 'karate film' and more than one Indian film, while restricting their release to a maximum of five weeks, regardless of the films' earnings.[15] Why did these decrees primarily target Indian and Hong Kong films? American or European productions were not intended for the same audience and did not threaten Egyptian films in the same way: 'Egyptian cinema began to feel a serious shortage of capital precisely when Indian films became a threat to the markets in which the local product was most effectively marketed.'[16]

This series of measures put an end to the expansion of Indian films on Egyptian screens.

Only a handful of Indian films circulated sporadically in the 1970s, until a major Indian film importer took over distribution in the 1980s and contributed to what has been considered the golden age of Hindi cinema in Egypt.[17] However, the Egyptian government did this to protect their film industry, which had suffered since nationalisation in 1963, and to preserve 'morals' which were at stake.

In 1980s Egypt, the popularity of Hindi films in cinemas fuelled the video market. The consumption patterns of these films developed at the intersection between public and private space. Although Indian films gradually disappeared from cinemas in Egypt, this actually marked the beginning of a broader entry of Hindi films into Arab homes, thanks to the development of VHS tapes and satellite TV channels.

16.
Armbrust, 'The Ubiquitous Nonpresence of India. Peripheral Visions from Egyptian Popular Culture', in Sangita Gopal and Sujata Moorti (ed.), *Global Bollywood: Travels of Hindi Song and Dance*, University of Minnesota Press, Minneapolis, 2008, p. 200–220.

17.
Dimitris Eleftheriotis and Dina Iordanova (ed.), *South Asian Popular Culture*, 'Indian Cinema Abroad: Historiography of Transnational Cinematic Exchanges', vol. 4, no. 2, Oxford, Routledge, 2006.

Fig. 36   Cinema Miami in 1991, Cairo

'Even after their popularity peaked, Oriental fantasy films inspired filmmakers to such an extent that a new film genre emerged: films of "Islamicate cultures".'

Bollywood and Its Orient Factory: Oriental Fantasy Films

NÉMÉSIS SROUR

In Bombay (present-day Mumbai), 1955, a film critic ridicules the film studios' craze for Oriental-Arabian imagery. In *Hoor-e-Arab* (1955) by Prem Narayan Arora [fig. 37], he noticed this contagious buzz: 'Of late all roads have been leading to Arabia and the latest in the industry to join the desert-bound caravan is Producer-director P N Arora [...]'. Drawing on all the stereotypes of the genre, the film recounts a love story set in the heart of the Arab royal court: 'all the typical characters of this sort of film, the bedridden Sultan, his fighting sons, the sleazy vizier and the enchanting Bedouin female dancer, are back in a pleasant potpourri of dances and duels, murders and mayhem, plots and counterplots of sly courtiers.'[1]

Inspired by *One Thousand and One Nights*, the Oriental fantasy film genre was very popular in India between the 1910s and 1930s. These films, however, are missing from the national narrative of film history. At the origins of Indian cinema, one name holds a place in history, Dadasaheb Phalke. In 1913, Phalke released *Raja Harishchandra* (*King Harishchandra*), the first Indian fiction film. With this film, he introduced the new and popular mythological genre in Indian cinema, which brought to life the stories of Hindu gods and goddesses. Hailed by the state government, the Bombay film industry, and the popular press[2] as the 'father of Indian cinema', Phalke alone epitomised the noble national cinema.[3] Yet, in his shadow lies Hiralal Sen, a forgotten pioneer

1.
Filmfare, 13 May 1955, p. 21.

2.
Tejaswini Ganti, *Bollywood: A Guidebook to Popular Hindi Cinema*, New York/London, Routledge, 2004.

3.
Emmanuel Grimaud, *Bollywood Film Studio ou comment les films se font à Bombay*, Paris, CNRS éditions, 2003.

4.
Rosie Thomas, *Bombay Before Bollywood: Film City Fantasies*, Albany, SUNY Press, 2013.

of Indian cinema history. At the turn of the 20th century, Sen's films featured the Arab-Persian world of *One Thousand and One Nights*, a very different cultural universe from mythological films. In the early decades of Indian cinema, these two kinds of cinema were simultaneously being developed and disseminated. The first belonged to mainstream culture, its films drawing inspiration from Hindu mythology; the other, related to an exotic Arab-Persian imaginary, was considered as a kind of popular entertainment, an entertainment for the masses.

The lack of exposure to Hiralal Sen's films is also due to the scarcity of archives and materials to tell their story. One must rely on secondary sources to trace its history. Among the films that are known, is a complete filmed version of an *Ali Baba* play, with close-ups and panoramic shots, edited to become a more than two-hour-long film, which is said to have been screened in cinemas in 1903 and 1904. However, in 1917, the warehouse, where these films were stored, burned down, destroying an entire chapter of film history. According to Film Historian Rosie Thomas, if the stories about Hiralal Sen's films are accurate, this would mean that the first Indian film was actually based on a tale from *One Thousand and One Nights*.[4] In the absence of any material evidence of the existence of Sen's film and its actual status as a film, along with the impossibility of assessing the work and its significance, since it was apparently a filmed play, film historians have either ignored it or dismissed it as mere footage of a Bengali theatre success. In any case, the works inspired by the stories from *One Thousand and One Nights* shed light on another dimension of Indian cinema, that of a lesser-known history, with hybrid visual forms.

Even after their popularity peaked, Oriental fantasy films inspired filmmakers to such an extent that a new film genre emerged: films of 'Islamicate cultures'.[5] Islamicate culture in cinema is characterised by narrative motifs derived from Persian stories, singing traditions such as *qawwali*, a genre of Sufi devotional music, or poetic forms such as the *ghazal*,

5.
Ira Bhaskar and Richard Allen (ed.), *Islamicate Cultures of Bombay Cinema*, New Delhi, Tulika Books, 2009.

a kind of love song. In these Hindi films, cities like Agra or Lucknow epitomise the urban Islamic imaginary and shots of the Agra Fort or the Taj Mahal convey a sense of nostalgia for past Muslim grandeur.

This imagery is not only restricted to films featuring 'Islamicate cultures' but is infused in Hindi cinema as a whole. These films would eventually fuel the standard imagery of cities in the Arab world, until the convergence of the Bombay and Dubai film industries which would help to dust off this frozen Orientalist image, as shown in Farah Khan's film *Happy New Year* (2014). When Bollywood leaves the studios, the exotic Orient is transformed and deconstructed, reshaped by natural settings.

Fig. 37　Poster for the film *Hoor-e-Arab* (1955), directed by Prem Narayan Arora

'The world of cinema is regularly integrated into the works of contemporary Indian artists in a supplementary way, and is mainly used as a tool to critique Indian society.'

Bollywood and the Indian Contemporary Scene

JEANNE RETHACKER

Since the 1990s, contemporary art from the Indian subcontinent has sought to distance itself from the stereotypes of 'indianness' that the West tends to ascribe to it.[1] Mughal miniatures and traditional paintings, which are usually associated with Indian art, do not belong to the vocabulary of these artists. Instead, the contemporary Indian socio-political context – economic openness, globalisation, the rising of fundamentalism, colonisation, and the Partition – is a far more important source of inspiration. According to Betty Seid, these artists use a 'narrative impulse' – to this day a key aspect of Indian cultural identity – to convey political and social contexts. They draw on traditional storytelling and 'expound, dramatise and regale us with stories.'[2] Many artists born from the 1950s onwards, also embraced new subjects, such as gender, globalisation, and consumerism. Since they did not experience colonial India, their work is less rooted in classical Indian history and culture than the previous generations of artists. Their artistic language is increasingly international while tackling local societal issues, and their techniques are new and diverse, though often reminiscent of vernacular processes and mediums – the studio photographs of Pushpamala N are a good example.

1.
Betty Seid, 'New Narratives', in Betty Seid (ed.), *New Narratives: Contemporary Art from India*, exh. cat., Ahmedabad: Mapin Publishing/Chicago: Chicago Cultural Center, 2007, p. 13.

2.
Ibid.

3.
Johan Pijnappel, 'Indian Video Art and the New Narrative Matrix', in Betty Seid, *op. cit.*, p. 26.

4.
In Indian culture, *hijras* are third-gender people, neither men nor women.

5.
'Her desire was to become a South Indian film star and see herself in a song and dance sequence, romancing the hero and to be romanced by him.' Tejal Shah, cited on the website of the Brooklyn Museum, New York (https://www.brooklynmuseum.org/eascfa/about/feminist_art_base/tejal-shah).

PARODYING BOLLYWOOD: REINVENTING STEREOTYPES

Reacting to the rapid changes in Indian society, many artists from the subcontinent began to explore new media in the 1990s. Audio-visual art and installations were widely developed by artists such as Nalini Malani, a true pioneer in the field of new media and video in India, as well as by Vivan Sundaram, Navjot Altaf, and Sheba Chhachhi. Video art in India mostly involved single screens, and shared common features with Indian film or television, although the content sharply diverges from the narrative style of Bollywood films.[3] However, Feminist Artist Tejal Shah drew her inspiration loosely from a Hindi film story in *Stinging Kiss* (2000). In an ironic yet provocative way, the artist reverses the roles of men and women in a drama that re-enacts a classic Hindi film abduction story, where she plays the role of the kidnaping thug. Her works are often parodies and play upon societal mores, imitating, for instance, stereotypes and the fantasy world of Bollywood fiction, to raise gender issues or the representation of minorities. In Shah's photographic series entitled Hijra Fantasy,[4] each model chose to embody an imaginary character. In *Southern Siren – Maheshwari* (2006, **fig. 39**), the model posed as a film star.[5] The image references popular Indian cinema: the heroine and her suitor occupy the centre of the composition in a typical dance posture, the setting is devoid of any external or urban elements; the dramatic arrangement suggests a dreamlike scene. Similarly, the flowers depicted in this work also evoke Bollywood symbolism, where the act of touching a flower represents a kiss.[6]

REFERENCING INDIAN CINEMA: A POLITICAL AND SOCIAL CRITIQUE

Television and cinema are an integral part of modern India's visual and cultural language. They are ubiquitous. Therefore, the world of cinema is regularly integrated into the works of contemporary Indian artists in a supplementary way, and is mainly used as a tool to critique Indian society. For instance, in her video/shadow play installation *Transgressions* (2001), Nalini Malani combines colourful excerpts from Bollywood films with Kalighat paintings, the Hindu goddess Durga, and two boxers who represent the continuous struggle between India and Pakistan. In his diptych *Bullet Shot in the Stomach* (2001), Bhupen Khakhar alludes to the 'double role', where the same actor plays both the hero and the anti-hero. Similar to a Bollywood movie poster, the artist portrays himself twice in this humorous, yet dark work – Khakhar was diagnosed with cancer at the time – one of his avatars points a gun at the other. The work of Sheba Chhachhi also draws inspiration from the history of film and television. As a feminist artist with works that are critical of contemporary Indian society, she denounces the stereotypes of Hindi cinema, and the machismo and violence inherent in them. In *Warrior/Saint* (2002), Chhachhi projects brutal images from macho films onto a man's white collared shirt containing an image of the Buddha in its pocket. Thus, she plays with the contrast between the pacifist figure of the Buddha and the violence of popular Indian cinema.[7]

6.
Pooja Padgaonkar, 'Shining a Spotlight on the Marginalized: Tejal Shah's Photographic Representation of the Hijra Community in India', *TCNJ Journal of Student Scholarship*, Volume XVII, Spring 2015.

7.
Henry-Claude Cousseau, Deepak Ananth, Jany Lauga (eds.), *Indian Summer, la jeune scène artistique indienne*, exh. cat., Paris: École nationale supérieure des beaux-arts, 2005, p. 46.

8.
Deepak Ananth, 'Atul Dodiya', in Sophie Duplaix and Fabrice Bousteau (eds.), *Paris-Delhi-Bombay...*, exh. cat., Paris: Centre Pompidou, 2011, p. 180.

POP CULTURE

The work of Atul Dodiya captures the everyday life of contemporary urban India, drawing inspiration from the megalopolis of Bombay (present-day Mumbai) and its ubiquitous visual culture. In his work, the artist superimposes images from Indian and Western popular culture, Bollywood blockbuster posters, as well as kitsch, mythological, political, and autobiographical images, or he references art history. Dodiya thwarts the classical rules of painting and the 'opposition between visual arts and popular culture',[8] while demonstrating the importance of references. A cinema enthusiast, Dodiya repeatedly uses Bollywood iconography in his work. In his self-portrait entitled *Bombay Buccaneer* (1994), he took inspiration from the film poster for *Baazigar* (*The Gambler*, 1993), directed by brothers Abbas Alibhai and Mastan Alibhai Burmawalla, where he included artistic references: Bhupen Khakhar and David Hockney reflected in the artist's glasses instead of film actresses. In *Gabbar on Cambodge* (1997, fig. 38), he reworked the figure of the criminal of Ramesh Sippy's *Sholay* (1975), one of the most popular Hindi films of the 20th century, surrounding him with morbid and violent images, thus creating a metaphorical work critical of both Indian society and of the glorification of violence in cinema. The colours used in the painting also evoke the Bollywood posters that adorn the city of Bombay with their gaudy palette. In the series Saptapadi: Scenes from a Marriage (Regardless) (2004), whose title refers to a part of a traditional Hindu wedding ceremony, images are juxtaposed on canvases. Their appearance recalls the kitsch iconography of the traditional hand-painted posters of popular Indian cinema. In *Charu* [fig. 42], a pop-style work from this series, Atul Dodiya brings together the figures of Western actresses – Brigitte Bardot (in Jean-Luc Godard's *Contempt*, 1963), Jeanne Moreau (in Michelangelo Antonioni's *La Notte* [*The Night*], 1961), and Liv Ullmann (in Ingmar Bergman's *Scenes from a Marriage*, 1973) – with that of Indian actress Madhavi Mukherjee (in Satyajit Ray's film *The Lonely Wife* [*Charulata*], 1964, fig. 19).

STUDIO PHOTOGRAPHY: MEMORY OF THE GOLDEN AGE OF INDIAN CINEMA

Since the mid-1990s, Pushpamala N has adopted photography as a medium. In her work, she uses multiple Indian societal and iconographic forms in an almost ethnographic manner. In her studio photographs – inspired by traditional studio portrait photography, which was immensely popular in India from the 1870s onwards – referred to as 'photo-performances',[9] the artist embodies several female characters from Indian culture, staging herself in typical costumes and settings. Pushpamala N subverts and parodies the chosen characters in kitschy and sentimental settings. In the series Native Women of South India: Manners and Customs (2000–2004, fig. 40) or The Navarasa Suite (2003, fig. 41), she plays with cultural stereotypes – middle-class tastes, Indian cinematic forms, or Anglo-Indian colonial aesthetics – and addresses the status of women in India. In the first series, created in collaboration with British photographer Clare Arni, she embodies typologies specific to South Indian women, using iconographies from both fine art and popular culture, as well as

9.
Susie Tharu, 'This is not an Inventory: Norm and Performance in Everyday Femininity', in Pushpamala N and Clare Arni (eds.), *Native Women of South India: Manners and Customs*, exh. cat., New Delhi: Nature Morte/New York: Bose Pacia/Mumbai: Gallery Chemould, 2007.

10.
Ravi Varma has remained an important source of inspiration and reference in modern and contemporary Indian art. In addition to Pushpamala N, Nalini Malani used the work *A Galaxy of Musicians* (1889) in her installation entitled *Unity in Diversity* (2003).

11.
Pushpamala N quoted on her website (http://www.pushpamala.com/projects/bombay-photo-studio-2003/).

12.
The Australian actress Mary Ann Evans – aka Fearless Nadia – was one of the first women to take the lead role in an Indian film with *Hunterwali*.

documentary-style illustrations. She references votive images of Hindu goddesses, anthropomorphic photographs, scenes from Indian films and paintings by Ravi Varma – religious subjects illustrating Hindu epics and gods, as well as his academic aesthetics, are a deep inspiration for her.[10] In her series Bombay Photo Studio (2003), Pushpamala N examines the work of Jethalal H Thakker, who established his India Photo Studio near the famous Chitra Cinema in Bombay in the late 1940s, where he immortalised the greatest stars of the golden age of Hindi cinema. Most active in the 1950s and 1960s, he was one of the first Bollywood photographers to implement a chiaroscuro-like technique, creating a dramatising effect in the photographs. In this series, Pushpamala N revisits this expressionist lighting technique, using Thakker's 'baroque style' to explore a 'neglected history of Indian photography, which deals with fantasy and storytelling rather than realism'.[11] Thus, Pushpamala N repeatedly uses the Bollywood aesthetic, in a humorous, documentary, or dramatic fashion. This reference can also be found in her films, particularly in *Phantom Lady* (1996–1998), for which she drew inspiration from the iconic Fearless Nadia[12] and her role as a masked adventuress in *Hunterwali* (1935), directed by Homi Wadia.

Fig. 39   Tejal Shah (born 1979). *Southern Siren – Maheshwari* from the series Hijra Fantasy. 2006. Digital photograph. 146 × 96.5 cm

Fig. 40   Pushpamala N (born 1956) in collaboration with Clare Arni (born 1962). *The Native Types/Flirting* from the series Native Women of South India: Manners and Customs. 2004. C-print. 76.2 × 50.8 cm

Fig. 42   Atul Dodiya (born 1959). *Charu* from the series Saptapadi: Scenes from Marriage (Regardless). 2004. Enamel paint and synthetic varnish on plywood. 183 × 122 cm. Paris, Centre Georges Pompidou, Musée National d'Art Moderne, Inv. AM 2013-293

Selected Biographies of Filmmakers and Actors

HÉLÈNE KESSOUS

Raj Kapoor
1924–1988

Yash Chopra
1932–2012

The son of Indian film pioneer Prithviraj Kapoor, Raj was an actor, filmmaker and producer. He was a key figure in the Hindi film industry that he helped shape with his studio R K Films. An icon from the golden age of Indian cinema, he is still remembered for his character of a beggar, very much inspired by Chaplin's Tramp. This character is featured in *The Vagabond (Awaara*, 1951) and *Shree 420* (1955), whose childish refrain, one of the hit songs, 'Mera Joota Hai Japani',[1] sung by this compassionate hero, conceals a profound social statement. Raj Kapoor represented India at the Cannes Film Festival with *Awaara* in 1953, but the film's reception was rather lukewarm; its length and the use of music and songs puzzled the French film critics, who failed to appreciate the poetry of this very different type of cinema. Raj Kapoor often stood in front of and behind the camera. He never ceased to develop his style, evolving from black and white to colour, brilliantly reinventing himself and always in tune with the times. In 1964, he made his mark on audiences with *Sangam*, a powerful melodrama whose plot intertwined the stories of a love triangle and a dangerous mission in Kashmir. In the 1970s, he made a series of films revolving around female characters, one of which was the mesmerising *The Truth, the God, the Beauty* (1978), starring his brother Shashi Kapoor. Beyond the impact he made on the history of Indian cinema with unforgettable emotional melodramas whose musical beat is still hummed today, Raj Kapoor was also the founder of a dynasty of actors, directors, and producers that continues to be one of the pillars of the Bollywood industry.

1.
'mera juta hai japani ye patalun imgalistani sar pe lal topi rusi phir bhi dil hai hindustani' 'My shoe is Japanese, my trousers are English, I have a Russian hat on my head, but my heart is Indian.'

A monumental figure in popular Hindi cinema and much more than a successful filmmaker, Yash Raj Chopra is one of the inventors and cornerstones of Bollywood cinema. The standardisation of themes that he cherished, such as love and friendship are due to Chopra, but also an array of visual codes and an aesthetic language that he never ceased to develop, refine, and establish. He was a star-maker, a trendsetter and ruled over Bollywood for decades. Known for his glamorous films, the 'king of romance' established his modernity and unconventionality, especially through scripts advocating love marriage in India where arranged marriages prevailed. Even more significant, he was the one who relocated romance narratives outside of India, creating a powerful link between Bollywood films and the Swiss Alps. Indeed, as a native of Lahore, in the heart of what is now Pakistan's Punjab region, he tirelessly filmed the Swiss green valleys and snow-capped mountains as symbols of his paradise lost. Among his greatest achievements are the dramatic *Dust's Flower* (1959), or the songless thriller *Coincidence* (1969), complicated love triangles and quadrilaterals with *Daag*, *Chandni*, and *Silsila*, featuring Amitabh Bachchan, his wife Jaya, and the inflammatory Rekha. He also indulged in lighter films with *Dil To Pagal Hai*, which, with its schoolboy sense of humour, veers clearly towards the American sitcom. But he truly excelled in taking the audience into the depths of thwarted love, and his odes to romantic sacrifices, such as *Veer-Zaara* (2004) and *As Long as I Live* (2012) – a posthumous film made as a last creative inspiration – remind us that this outstanding filmmaker relentlessly pursued the capture and depiction of every shade of love throughout his career.

Amitabh Bachchan
Born 1942

Rajinikanth
Born 1950

Amitabh Bachchan, also known as the *Shahensha* (the king of kings), was born in Allahabad. His father, Harivansh Rai, was a remarkable poet and his mother, Teji, was a renowned social activist. A leading actor in the Bollywood scene, Bachchan, 'Big B', and the myth surrounding him was forged in the 1970s. A modern-day hero, he embodied a new sort of *jeune premier*: 'the angry young man', a persona he developed through blockbusters such as *Shackles* (1973) by Prakash Mehra, *The Wall* (1975) by Yash Chopra, and *Sholay* (1975) by Ramesh Sippy. In these spectacular action films, Bachchan emerged as the champion of the oppressed against a corrupt system. From the mid-1970s onwards, his roles became more diverse which enabled him to become a superstar who could play anything: a romantic poet, a loving brother, or a caring husband. From these roles, he became a legend and never stopped reinventing himself over the course of an incredibly long career. In the 2000s, he started anew by tirelessly playing the roles of patriarchs, which were, in some cases, benevolent or at other times, icy and inflexibly dogmatic. Audiences enjoyed seeing him alongside rising stars, since acting in a film with him was perceived to be an endorsement. With over two hundred films under his belt spanning five decades, four Filmfare Awards as Best Actor, as well as a Dadasaheb Phalke Award for lifetime achievement, Amitabh Bachchan deserves his finest nickname: the *sadi ke mahanayak* (the great actor of the century).

Words cannot describe the fervour generated by this celebrated Kollywood actor, producer, and screenwriter. Referred to by his fans as *thailavar* (the leader), he launched his career in the second half of the 1970s, alternating between films in Tamil, Telugu, and Kannada. He gradually gained success while performing Amitabh Bachchan's roles in Tamil remakes of Hindi films such as *Billa* (1980) by R Krishnamurthy, a remake of *Don*. Thus, he became 'the angry young man' of South India, a symbol of the people's struggle against injustice. He soon developed his own style, which made him an inimitable figure of the film scene. It was in the film *Three Faces* (1982) by A Jagannathan, that he first performed several characters, something that was to become his trademark. Each of his appearances rivalled each other in cleverness and special effects, with a tremendous amount of wigs and make-up, which made his performances more spectacular each time. Due to his popularity, he made films in North India, the first of which, *Blind Law* (1983) by Rama Rao Tatineni, he starred alongside Amitabh Bachchan and Hema Malini. In the 1990s, his films broke audience records, as far away as Japan with his film *Pearl* (1995) by K S Ravikumar. Like many actors of his generation, the 2000s pushed him to reinvent himself to maintain his position in a rapidly evolving cinema. His role as a superhero in *Robot* (2010) by S Shankar [fig. 33], or the motion capture film *Kochadaiiyaan* (2014) by Soundarya Rajinikanth Vishagan, come to mind, which position him in a popular cinema receptive to new themes and technologies. Yet another example that nothing is impossible for Rajinikanth who continues to enthral his fans.

Zeenat Aman
Born 1951

Mani Ratnam
Born 1956

In India, beauty queens often become actresses, and Zeenat Aman is a prime example. This Miss Asia Pacific International was adored by the industry from her first appearances in 1970, even though her first two features, *Commotion* (1971) by O P Ralhan, and *Ruckus* (1971) by S M Abbas, were complete flops. She found her audience with the film *Haré Rama Haré Krishna* (1971) by Dev Anand, and stole the show in the iconic *Procession of Memories* (1973), a Nasir Hussain masterpiece. It was one of the early films of the *masala* genre[2] that also ushered in the Bollywood era. Generations of moviegoers still remember Zeenat Aman's performances in 'Dum Maro Dum' and 'Churaliya yeh tumne jo dil ko', the hit songs of these two films. The actress shook up the traditional codes of femininity by appearing in casual outfits, with her hair loose, and her unique modern look. She made headlines with her role as Rupa in *The Truth, the God, the Beauty* (1978) by Raj Kapoor, co-starring Shashi Kapoor, the director's brother. The film was accused of doublespeak, since the story, which was supposed to promote the beauty of the soul, was constructed by ostensibly filming the actress's attractive and scantily-clad body. That same year, she starred in *Don* (1978) by Chandra Barot, alongside Amitabh Bachchan. Despite a short career, Zeenat Aman left a mark on Bollywood history, blurring the line between the vamp and the perfect woman.

2.
Masala literally means 'mixture of spices' and can be more or less spicy. This culinary metaphor is often used to describe the mix of genres that is so distinctive in Bollywood films.

Nothing destined this unclassifiable filmmaker, Mani Ratnam, to pursue a career in cinema. Neither a commercial nor an auteur director, he oscillated between films in Hindi and in Tamil, and has built, over the course of his career, a unique cinematic world and aesthetic. His first films in the 1980s were mostly critical and commercial failures, except for the success of *Mouna Ragam* (1986), whose realism appealed to audiences. It was not until the 1990s that he achieved even greater accolades, thanks to his career-defining Terrorism Trilogy consisting of *Rose* (1992), *Bombay* (1995) and *From the Heart* (1998). Ratnam established himself as a storyteller of reality, although he did not overlook the visual power of popular cinema's musical sequences. In the 2000s, he continued to make films that addressed sensitive issues, such as *Kannathil Muthamittal*, which tells the story of a Sri Lankan Tamil adopted child in India who longs to be reunited with her biological mother while a civil war rages on the island. In fact, Ratnam did not limit himself to one film style: in 2007, he directed *Guru*, a breathtaking Bollywood film featuring Aishwarya Rai and Abhishek Bachchan. The financial resources allocated to the filming of this blockbuster enabled him to perfect and sublimate his cinematic aesthetic. In 2010, he made two versions of a film with different actors based on Ravana, the demon of the mythological epic *Ramayana*. With *Raavanan* (Tamil) and *Raavan* (Hindi), the filmmaker explored the nuances of this cultural antihero. Mani Ratnam holds an exceptional position that distinguishes him as a director of popular films who manages to interweave North and South India, politics and emotion, romance and revolt, combined with the utmost attention to music.

Sanjay Leela Bhansali
Born 1963

Sanjay Leela Bhansali is an authoritative director, screenwriter and composer of popular Hindi cinema. He achieved success very early in his career with his second film, *Hum Dil de Chuke Sanam* (1999), which starred Aishwarya Rai, Salman Khan, and Ajay Devgan. However, he made his mark with the virtuosity of *Devdas* (2002). By opening the Cannes Film Festival, the film put Bollywood in the spotlight of the international Western scene, for a time. Since then, Bhansali is known as a master of colour, majestic sets, and mesmerising choreography. In 2005, he experimented with a new genre in *Black*, a film in which he also composed the music. Drawing inspiration from the life of Helen Keller, Bhansali made a radical change in his style, and the film became a huge success in India. After two critical and commercial failures, *My Love* (2007) and *Request* (2010), he had success again in 2013 with *Goliyon Ki Rasleela Ram-Leela*, an adaptation of *Romeo and Juliet*. A symbol of generational change, the film is beautifully performed by Ranveer Singh and Deepika Padukone, the new star couple. This duo performed again in his next two films, *Bajirao Mastani* (2015) and *Padmaavat* (2018, **fig. 18**). In these two opuses, the director brought his art of setting and dramaturgy to a climax, transforming historical-mythological films into true works of art. In 2022, *Gangubai Kathiawadi* glorifies the struggle of a neighbourhood of prostitutes, combining ruthlessness with an exacerbated aestheticism. As a master of flamboyant Bollywood, Bhansali pursues – as much as he revolutionises – the history of popular cinema.

Salman Khan
Born 1965

Salman Khan, the son of screenwriter Salim Khan, made his debut in the late 1980s. He became successful from his first lead role in *I've Loved* (1989) by Sooraj R Barjatya, in which he established his trademark: his muscles. In addition to an immensely successful career, Salman Khan revolutionised the Indian actor's representation by pioneering the image of a hairless, muscular body. Associated with this new masculinity, Salman Khan's image was disseminated all over India, especially in gyms, where young men sought to shape their bodies to match that of their idol, whom they nicknamed *Bhai*, i.e., big brother. An unclassifiable actor, he has played in romantic comedies such as *Hum Dil De Chuke Sanam* (1999) by Sanjay Leela Bhansali, co-starring with Aishwarya Rai, as well as in films addressing strong social issues, such as a couple with infertility and the use of surrogate mothers in *Secretly and Stealthily* (2001) by Abbas Alibhai Burmawalla and Mastan Alibhai Burmawalla, or the place of women in high-performance sports and more generally in Indian society with *Sultan* (2016) by Ali Abbas Zafar. He is a scandalous figure in Hindi cinema, and his bad-boy reputation has followed him off the screen.

Shah Rukh Khan
Born 1965

Shah Rukh Khan, also known as SRK, is a prominent Bollywood actor and producer. His nicknames, the *Baadshah* (emperor) of Bollywood, or 'King Khan', perfectly reflect his position within the star system. However, since he did not come from a prominent film family, no one could predict that SRK would become such a star. In the late 1980s, he landed his first role in *Solider*, a realistic television series, where he played an ordinary man. Different from the great actors who preceded him, Shah Rukh Khan did not have the appearance nor the fair complexion of the *jeune premier* that Bollywood loved so much, but from his debut, the public was not mistaken and appreciated the innovation he brought to a very formatted industry. His film career started in the early 1990s with two pivotal roles as an antagonist, a bold move in Bollywood. He portrayed a murderer in *The Gambler* (1993) by Abbas Alibhai Burmawalla and Mastan Alibhai Burmawalla, and an obsessive lover in *Fear* (1993) by Yash Chopra. It was on the set of *The Gambler* that he first appeared with the actress Kajol, who was to become his film partner. During the 1990s and early 2000s, he starred in very popular romantic comedies. Since then, this unrivalled Prince Charming, who ruled over popular Hindi cinema for more than twenty years, has been reinventing himself, with varying degrees of success, in an effort to keep his title of 'emperor of Indian cinema'.

Madhuri Dixit
Born 1967

Actress Madhuri Dixit is acclaimed for her beauty, dancing skills, and her strong characters. With a prolific career, she starred in more than seventy films and received six Filmfare Awards, four of them for Best Actress. Dixit made her debut in 1984 with the leading role in *The Innocent* (1984) by Hiren Nag and, after several years hindered by commercial failures, she made her mark with the action film *Acid* (1988) by N Chandra. While she continued to appear in this film genre (*Villain* by Subhash Ghai, 1993), she subsequently gained prominence in the 1990s by playing lead roles in romantic blockbusters such as *Heart* (1990) by Indra Kumar, *Hum Aapke Hain Koun...!* (1994) by Sooraj R Barjatya, and *Dil To Pagal Hai* (1997) by Yash Chopra, in which she co-starred with SRK. In 2002, before stepping away from the star system for a few years, she stole the show in Sanjay Leela Bhansali's *Devdas* with Aishwarya Rai and SRK. She returned to the limelight in 2007 with the film *Come, Let's Dance* by Anil Mehta. Due to her talent, Madhuri Dixit still has a place today in a film industry that gives little space to women characters and actresses in their fifties. She appeared for instance in *Kalank* (2019) by Abhishek Varman and stars in the Netflix series *The Fame Game* (2022).

Karan Johar
Born 1972

As the son of a producer, Karan Johar belongs to the inner circle of the industry. He began his career as an actor before becoming a director, producer (Dharma Production), and TV talk show presenter. In 1995, he assisted Director Aditya Chopra, his cousin and the son of filmmaker Yash Chopra, on the set of *Dilwale Dulhania Le Jayenge* (1995). With his first film, *Something Happens* (1998), he followed in the footsteps of the Chopra family to such an extent that it is said that the Chopra-Johar system is a key element of Bollywood's visual language. Indeed, all the ingredients for success were gathered: young actors on the verge of becoming superstars (Kajol, SRK, or Rani Mukerji), bewitching music and choreography infused with modern jazz. *Sometimes There Is Joy, Sometimes There Is Sorrow...* (2001), an ensemble film with a dazzling cast, established his status as an influential and unusual director whose films are eagerly awaited by audiences. He is also a successful producer; Dharma Production has pushed the boundaries of Bollywood with films such as *Friendship* (2008), which deals with homosexuality, *Kapoor & Sons* (2016) and *Dear Zindegi* (2016), which have reinvented the genre and the form of popular film. In fewer than ten feature-length films, Karan Johar has embodied a distinct notation of Indian modernity and society. Even though he remains conservative in many respects, he addresses taboo subjects such as adultery, divorce, and female desire.

Aishwarya Rai Bachchan
Born 1973

Aishwarya Rai Bachchan is definitely the most international of Indian stars. After being crowned Miss World 1994 at the age of 21 and becoming a brand ambassador for L'Oréal, she debuted in 1997 in *The Duo*, a Tamil film directed by Mani Ratnam, and then in ...*And Love Happened* (1997) by Rahul Rawail, a Hindi film co-starring Bobby Deol. Her popularity quickly grew thanks to her roles in late 1990s blockbusters such as *Jeans* (1998) by S Shankar, or *Hum Dil De Chuke Sanam* (1999) by Sanjay Leela Bhansali, with Salman Khan, until the breakout film *Devdas* which opened the Cannes Film Festival in 2002. Aishwarya Rai has appeared in both North and South Indian films working with the greatest actors and directors. She even made a notable foray into Bengali auteur cinema with the delicate *Chokker Bali* (2003) by Rituparno Gosh. In the 2000s, Rai experimented by acting in action films with *Dhoom:2* (2006) by Sanjay Gadhvi, in which she appeared alongside Hrithik Roshan. A few years later, she starred with him again in *Jodhaa Akbar* (2008) by Ashutosh Gowariker [**fig. 17**], which is one of her most beautiful and successful roles to this day. After a career break to focus on her family, Aishwarya Rai Bachchan made a lukewarm comeback in the film *Ae Dil Hai Mushkil* (2016) by Karan Johar, in which she plays a woman in a relationship with a younger man. Turning away from critics who blamed her for not having lost her pregnancy weight, 'Aish' demonstrated her willingness to play mature women, breaking free from convention. Since then, she has sought to develop unique roles in an Indian cinema that is often stifled by outdated female stereotypes.

Kajol
Born 1974

Kajol is the daughter of Director Shomu Mukherjee and Actress Tanuja. Like many actresses of the golden age of Bollywood before her, she decided to be called only by her first name. She began her career at a very young age and was noticed in her second film, *The Gambler* (1993), co-starring SRK. Shortly afterwards, they were cast together in *Dilwale Dulhania Le Jayenge* (1995) by Aditya Chopra, one of the biggest hits of the Indian film industry, which played for more than 25 years at the Maratha Mandir cinema in Bombay (present-day Mumbai). This film kicked off the cinematic success of the duo, which became, for a long time, one of the most mythical Bollywood couples. Far from contenting herself with her successful performances in classic romantic comedies, Kajol ventured into thrillers and comedies. When she plays the lead role in a major drama, she excels in her multifaceted acting ability, as in *Annihilation* (2006) by Kunal Kohli, where she plays both a young blind woman in love and a militant citizen opposed to a terrorist played by Aamir Khan. Throughout her career, she has played characters close to the people, which has been a crucial element of her popularity. Kajol is now the most decorated Indian actress by the Filmfare Awards Academy, breaking the record previously held by her aunt Nutan.

Bibliography

Javed Akhtar
Talking Films: Conversations on Hindi Cinema with Javed Akhtar, New Delhi/New York, Oxford University Press, Oxford India Paperbacks series, 2003.

Deepak Ananth
'Atul Dodiya', in Sophie Duplaix and Fabrice Bousteau (ed.), *Paris-Delhi-Bombay ...*, exhibition catalogue, Paris, Centre Pompidou, 25 May -19 September 2011, Paris, Éditions du Centre Pompidou, 2011.

Khalid Anis Ahmed (ed.)
Intercultural Encounter in Mughal Miniatures (Mughal-Christian miniatures), Lahore, National College of Arts, 1995.

Douglas Barrett and Basil Gray
La Peinture indienne, Geneva, Skira, Les Trésors de l'Asie series, 1963.

Marie-Claude Bénard
La Sortie au cinéma : palaces et ciné-jardins d'Égypte (1930-1980), Marseille, Éditions Parenthèses-MMSH, Parcours méditerranéens series, 2016.

Ira Bhaskar and Richard Allen (ed.)
Islamicate Cultures of Bombay Cinema, New Delhi, Tulika Books, 2009.

Nandini Bhattacharya
Hindi Cinema: Repeating the Subject, New York/London, Routledge, Intersections: Colonial and Postcolonial Histories series, 2013.

Someśvara Bhaumika
Indian Cinema, Colonial Contours, Kolkata, Papyrus, 1995.

Mihir Bose
Bollywood: A History, New Delhi, Roli Books, 2007.

Centre interarabe du cinéma et de la télévision
'Cinéma et cultures arabes. IVᵉ conférence de la table ronde organisée avec l'aide technique de l'Unesco', Beirut, 25 October 1965.

Sarat Chandra Chatterjee
Devdas, Paris, Les Belles Lettres, La Voix de l'Inde series, 2006.

Shoma A Chatterji
Subject Cinema, Object Women: A Study of the Portrayal of Women in Indian Cinema, Kolkata, Parumita Publications, 1998.

Rupika Chawla
Raja Ravi Varma: Painter of Colonial India, Ahmedabad, India Ocean Township, N J, Mapin Publishing, 2010.

Prem Chowdhry
Colonial India and the Making of Empire Cinema, Manchester, New York, Manchester University Press, 2000.

Ananda Kentish Coomaraswamy
Introduction to Indian Art, New Delhi, Munshiram Manoharial, 1966.

Jean-François Cornu and Raïssa Brégeat-Padamsee (ed.)
Indomania : le cinéma indien des origines à nos jours, Paris, Cinémathèque française, 1995.

Olivier Cousin
'Conservation et restauration des films Eastmancolor', *1895*, Revue d'histoire du cinéma, 1996, vol. 20, no 1, p. 81-98 .

Henry-Claude Cousseau Deepak Ananth, Jany Lauga (ed.)
Indian Summer, la jeune scène artistique indienne, Paris, École nationale supérieure des beaux-arts, 2005.

Rajashri Dasgupta, Charu Gargi and Nasreen Munni Kabir
Women in Indian Film, New Delhi, Zubaan, 2009.

Amandine D'Azevedo
Cinéma indien, mythes anciens, mythes modernes : résurgences, motifs esthétiques et mutations des mythes dans le film populaire hindi contemporain, PhD thesis, Université de la Sorbonne Nouvelle, Paris, France, 2014.

Amandine D'Azevedo
Mythes, films, bazar. Formes transversales des cinémas indiens, Milan, Mimésis, 2018.

Laura Dean
'Forget Hollywood, Egyptians Are in Love with Bollywood', Public Radio International, 17 May 2015 (online version: https://www.pri.org/stories/2015-05-17/forget-hollywood-egyptians-are-love-bollywood).

G Dhananjayan
Pride of Tamil Cinema 1931–2013: Tamil Films that Have Earned National and International Recognition, Madras, Blue Ocean Publishers, 2014.

G Dhananjayan
The Best of Tamil Cinema, 1931 to 2010: A Journey Through Eighty Years of Tamil Cinema from India, Madras, Galatta Media, 2010.

Rachel Dwyer
Filming the Gods, New York/London, Routledge, 2006.

Rachel Dwyer and Divia Patel
Cinema India: The Visual Culture of Hindi Film, London, Reaktion Books, Envisioning Asia series, 2002.

Rachel Dwyer and Jerry Pinto
Beyond the Boundaries of Bollywood, New Delhi/New York, Oxford University Press, South Asian Cinema series, 2011.

Diana L Eck
Darśan, Seeing the Divine Image in India, third edition, New York, Columbia University Press, 1996.

Dimitris Eleftheriotis and Dina Iordanova (ed.)
South Asian Popular Culture, 'Indian Cinema Abroad: Historiography of Transnational Cinematic Exchanges', vol. 4, no 2, Oxford, Routledge, 2006.

Wilber Theodore Elmore
Dravidian Gods in Modern Hinduism, 2nd edition, New Delhi, Asian Educational Services, 1995.

Swarnavel Eswaran Pillai
Madras Studios: Narrative, Genre, and Ideology in Tamil Cinema, New Delhi/Thousand Oaks, Sage Publications, 2015.

Térésa Faucon and Amandine D'Azevedo (ed.)
In/dépendance des cinémas indiens. Cartographie des formes, des genres et des régions, Paris, Presses Sorbonne Nouvelle, 2016.

Garret Fay
Studying Bollywood, Leighton Buzzard, Auteur Publishing, Studying Films series, 2011.

Tejaswini Ganti
Producing Bollywood inside the Contemporary Hindi Film Industry, Durham, Duke University Press, 2012.

Pramod Ganpatye
A Guide to the Indian Miniature, New Delhi, National Museum, 1994.

Tejaswini Ganti
Bollywood: A Guidebook to Popular Hindi Cinema, New York/London, Routledge, 2004.

Sharmistha Gooptu
Bengali Cinema: 'An Other Nation',
New York/London, Routledge, 2010.

**Sangita Gopal
and Sujata Moorti (ed.)**
*Global Bollywood: Travels of Hindi
Song and Dance*, Minneapolis,
University of Minnesota Press,
2008.

Emmanuel Grimaud
*Bollywood Film Studio ou comment
les films se font à Bombay*,
Paris, CNRS editions, Monde
indien series, 2003.

Tourya Guaaybess
*Télévisions arabes sur orbite :
un système médiatique en mutation
(1960-2004)*, Paris, CNRS Editions,
Connaissance du monde arabe
series, 2013.

John Guy
Indian Temple Sculpture, London,
V&A Publications, 2007.

Robert L Hardgrave, Jr
*When Stars Displace the Gods:
The Folk Culture of Cinema in Tamil
Nadu*, Austin, University of Texas,
Center for Asian Studies, 1975.

Youssef Ishaghpour
Satyajit Ray, l'Orient et l'Occident,
Paris, Éditions de La Différence,
Les Essais series, 2002.

Kajri Jain
*Gods in the Bazaar: The Economies
of Indian Calendar Art*, Durham,
Duke University Press, Objects/
histories series, 2007.

Madhu Jain
*The Kapoors: The First Family
of Indian Cinema*, New Delhi,
Penguin Books, 2009.

Sundar Kaali
'Narrating Seduction: Vicissitudes
of the Sexed Subject in Tamil
Nativity Film', in Ravi S. Vasudevan
(ed.), *Making Meaning in Indian
Cinema*, New Delhi/New York,
Oxford University Press, 2000,
p. 168–190.

Nasreen Munni Kabir (ed.)
Les Stars du cinéma indien, Paris,
Centre Pompidou and Centre
national de la cinématographie,
Cinéma/singulier series, 1985.

Nasreen Munni Kabir
Bollywood: The Indian Cinema Story,
London, Channel 4 Books, 2001.

Nasreen Munni Kabir
*The Dialogue of Raj Kapoor's Classic:
Awaara*, New Delhi, Niyogi Books, 2010.

**Raminder Kaur
and Ajay J Sinha (ed.)**
*Bollyworld: Popular Indian Cinema
Through a Transnational Lens*,
New Delhi/Thousand Oaks, Sage
Publications, 2005.

Mohamed Khalid
'Le cinéma indien et ses stars',
in Nasreen Munni Kabir (ed.),
Les Stars du cinéma indien, Paris,
Centre Pompidou and Centre
national de la cinématographie,
Cinéma/singulier series, 1985.

Lata Khubchandani
Raj Kapoor: The Great Showman,
New Delhi, Rupa Publications,
2003.

Francis L F Lee
'Bollywood and Globalization:
The Global Power of Popular Hindi
Cinema', *Asian Journal
of Communication*, 3 September
2014, vol. 24, no 5, p. 505–507.

Lisa A Lewis
*The Adoring Audience: Fan Culture
and Popular Media*, New York/London,
Routledge, 1992.

Sudhir Mahadevan
'Early Cinema in South Asia:
The Place of Technology in Narrative
of its Emergence', *Framework*,
vol. 54, no 2, Autumn 2013,
p. 140–145.

Karline McLain
*India's Immortal Comic Books
Gods, Kings, and Other Heroes*,
Bloomington/Indianapolis, Indiana
University Press, Contemporary
Indian Studies series, 2009.

Ananda Mitra
India Through the Western Lens,
New Delhi/Thousand Oaks,
Sage Publications, 1999.

**Annamaria Motrescu-Mayes
and Marcus Banks (ed.)**
Visual Histories of South Asia,
New Delhi, Primus Books, 2018.

Constantine V Nakassis
*Doing Style: Youth and Mass
Mediation in South India*, Chicago,
University of Chicago Press,
2016.

Ritu Nanda
Raj Kapoor: His Life and His Films,
Mumbai/Moscow, RK Films &
Studios/Iskusstvo Publishers, 1991.

Ashis Nandy
*The Secret Politics of Our Desires:
Innocence, Culpability and Indian
Popular Cinema*, London,
Zed Books Ltd, 1999.

**Erwin Neumayer
and Christine Schelberger**
*Popular Indian Art: Raja Ravi
Varma and the Printed Gods of India*,
New Delhi, Oxford University
Press, 2003.

Amina Okada
*Le Grand Moghol et ses peintres :
miniaturistes de l'Inde aux xvi^e
et xviie siècles*, Paris,
Flammarion, 1992.

**Amina Okada
and Roselyne Hurel**
*Pouvoir et Désir : miniatures indiennes
du San Diego Museum of Art*,
exhibition catalogue, Nice,
Musée des arts asiatiques,
23 November 2002 - 23 February 2003;
Geneva, Collections Baur,
20 March - 18 June 2003, Paris/
Suilly-la-Tour, Paris-Musées/Findakly,
Patrimoines d'orient series, 2002.

Pooja Padgaonkar
'Shining a Spotlight on the
Marginalized: Tejal Shah's
Photographic Representation
of the Hijra Community in India',
*TCNJ Journal of Student
Scholarship*, vol. XVII,
Spring 2015.

Jacob Pandian
*The Making of India and Indian
Traditions*, New Jersey,
Prentice Hall, 1995.

Édith Parlier-Renault
*La symbolique des couleurs dans
les miniatures râjpoutes*, in Pierre-
Sylvain Filliozat and Michel Zink (ed.),
'Voir et concevoir la couleur en Asie,
actes du colloque international
organisé par l'Académie des
Inscriptions et des Belles-Lettres
et l'Inalco', 11-12 January 2013, Paris,
Académie des Inscriptions et des
Belles-Lettres, 2016.

Jean-Loup Passek
Le Cinéma indien, Paris,
L'Équerre, Cinéma-pluriel series,
1983.

S K Patil
'The Year in Retrospect.
An Annual Survey of the Film
Industry by Leading Spokesmen',
Filmfare, 16 mars 1956, p. 6.

Heidi Pauwels
*The Goddess as Role Model:
Sītā and Rādhā in Scripture
and on Screen*, New York,
Oxford University Press, 2008.

Manjunath Pendakur
*Indian Popular Cinema: Industry,
Ideology and Consciousness*,
New York, Hampton Press, 2003.

Christopher Pinney
Photos of the Gods. The Printed Image and Political Struggle in India, London, Reaktion Books, 2004.

Jerry Pinto
Helen: The Life and Times of an H-Bomb, New Delhi/New York, Penguin Books, 2006.

Gehan Rachty and Khalil Sabat (ed.)
Importation of Films for Cinema and Television in Egypt: A Study, Paris, Unesco, Communication and society series, 1981.

M K Raghavendra
50 Indian Film Classics: From Prem Sanyas to Rang De Basanti... Fifty Must-See Films, New Delhi, Collins by HarperCollins Publishers India, 2009.

Ashish Rajadhyaksha
'The "Bollywoodization" of the Indian Cinema: Cultural Nationalism in a Global Arena', *Inter-Asia Cultural Studies*, 1 January 2003, vol. 4, no 1, pp. 25–39.

Ashish Rajadhyaksha
Encyclopaedia of Indian Cinema, New York/London, Routledge, 1999.

Anjali Ram,
Consuming Bollywood: Gender, Globalization and Media in the Indian Diaspora, New York, Peter Lang, 2014.

T M Ramachandran and S. Rukmini (ed.)
70 Years of Indian Cinema (1913–1983), New Delhi, Cinema India-International, 1985.

Naman Ramachandran
Rajinikanth: The Definitive Biography, New Delhi, Penguin Books India, 2012.

Sumathi Ramaswamy (ed.)
Beyond Appearances? Visual Practices and Ideologies in Modern India, New Delhi/Thousand Oaks, Sage Publications, 2003.

Sumathi Ramaswamy
Passions of the Tongue, Language Devotion in Tamil India, 1891–1970, Berkeley, University of California Press, 1997.

Shakuntala Rao
'The Globalization of Bollywood: An Ethnography of Non-Elite Audiences in India', *The Communication Review*, vol. 10, no 1, 2007, p. 57–76.

Satyajit Ray
Écrits sur le cinéma, Paris, Éditions Jean-Claude Lattès, 1982.

Satyajit Ray
J'aurais voulu pouvoir vous les montrer : conférences, notes de festivals, dessins, Sandip Ray (ed.), Paris, G3J Éditeur, 2016.

Satyajit Ray
Our Films, Their Films, Mumbai, Orient Longman Limited, 1976.

Anil Relia and Dr Ratan Parimoo
The Indian Portrait – Colonial Influence on Raja Ravi Varma and his Contemporaries, Gujarat, Archer, 2014.

Andrew Robinson
Satyajit Ray: The Inner Eye, Berkeley, University of California Press, 1989.

Anil Saari
Indian Cinema: the Faces Behind the Masks, New Delhi/New York, Oxford University Press, 2011.

Bhaskar Sarkar
Mourning of the Nation: Indian Cinema in the Wake of Partition, Durham/London, Duke University Press, 2009.

Kerry Segrave
American Films Abroad: Hollywood's Domination of the World's Movie Screens from the 1890s to the Present, Jefferson/London, McFarland, 1997.

Betty Seid (ed.)
New Narratives: Contemporary Art from India, exhibition catalogue, Chicago, Chicago Cultural Center, 20 July - 23 September 2007; Salina, Salina Art Center, 5 January - 16 March 2008; New Brunswick, Jane Voorhees Zimmerli Art Museum, 12 April - 31 July 2008, Ahmedabad, Mapin Publishing, 2007.

Catherine Servan-Schreiber
'Inde et Grande-Bretagne : deux regards sur un passé colonial à travers le cinéma', *Hermès, La Revue*, 2008, no 52, p. 25–32.

Tadashi Shimizu
The Bhāgavata-Purāna Miniature Paintings from the Bhandarkar Oriental Research Institute Manuscript dated 1648, Tokyo, The Centre for East Asian Cultural Studies for Unesco, the Toyo Bunko, Bibliotheca codicum Asiaticorum 7, 1993.

Jean Soustiel, Marie-Christine David, and Denise Glück
Miniatures orientales de l'Inde : les écoles et leurs styles, exhibition catalogue, Paris, 14-25 May 1973, Paris, Joseph Soustiel, 1973.

Jean Soustiel and Marie-Christine David
Miniatures orientales de l'Inde : écoles mogholes, du Deccan, et autres écoles indiennes. Présentation d'un ensemble de peintures musulmanes et rajpoutes appartenant à Joseph Soustiel, exhibition catalogue, Paris, 25 October — 8 November 1974, Paris, Joseph Soustiel, 1974.

Susan Stronge
Painting for the Mughal Emperor: The Art of the Book 1560–1660, London, V&A Publications, 2002.

Vaasanthi Sundaram
Rajinikanth: A Life, New Delhi, Aleph Book Co., 2021.

Charles Tesson
Satyajit Ray, Paris, Cahiers du cinéma, Auteurs series, 1992.

Susie Tharu
'This is not an Inventory: Norm and Performance in Everyday Femininity', in Pushpamala N and Clare Arni, *Native Women of South India: Manners and Customs*, exhibition catalogue, New Delhi, Nature Morte; New York, Bose Pacia; Mumbai, Gallery Chemould, 2007.

Rosie Thomas
Bombay before Bollywood: Film City Fantasies, Albany, State University of New York Press, Horizons of Cinema series, 2013.

Yves Thoraval
The Cinemas of India, Macmillan India Limited, New Delhi, 2000.

Jonathan Torgovnik and Nasreen Munni Kabir (ed.)
Bollywood Dreams: An Exploration of the Motion Picture Industry and its Culture in India, London, Phaidon Press, 2003.

Vālmīki
Rāmāyana, Paris, Diane de Selliers, 2011.

Aruna Vasudev
'Le nouveau cinéma indien', in Jean-François Cornu and Raïssa Brégeat-Padamsee (ed.), *Indomania : le cinéma indien des origines à nos jours*, Paris, Cinémathèque française, 1995.

Ravi S Vasudevan
'Addressing the Spectator of a "Third World" National Cinema: the Bombay "Social" Film of the 1940s and 1950s', *Screen*, Winter 1995, vol. 36, no 4, p. 305–324.

Charlotte Vaudeville (ed.)
Le Rāmāyan de Tulsī-dās,
Paris, Les Belles Lettres,
Le Monde indien series, 1977.

Selvaraj Velayutham (ed.)
*Tamil Cinema: The Cultural Politics
of India's Other Film Industry*,
New York/London, Routledge, 2008.

**Selvaraj Velayutham
and Vijay Devadas (ed.)**
*Tamil Cinema in the Twenty-First
Century: Caste, Gender
and Technology*, New York/
London, Routledge, 2021.

E M J Veniyoor
Raja Ravi Varma, Trivandrum,
Museums and Zoos and
Art Gallery, 1981.

Édouard Waintrop
'Bombay, Madras, Calcutta.
Le triangle d'or', in Jean-François
Cornu and Raïssa Brégeat-Padamsee
(ed.), *Indomania : le cinéma indien
des origines à nos jours*, Paris,
Cinémathèque française, 1995,
p. 149-156.

Richard Edmund Ward
*India's Pro-Arab Policy:
A Study in Continuity*, New York/
Westport/London, Praeger, 1992.

Ophélie Wiel
Bollywood et les Autres, Paris,
Buchet-Chastel, 2011.

Ophélie Wiel
Rendezvous with Hindi Cinema,
New Delhi, Sage Publications
India, 2011.

Bollywood Superstars: A Short Story of Indian Cinema

Edited by Julien Rousseau
and Hélène Kessous

Graphic design:
Coline Aguettaz

English translation:
Julie Higonnet
(The Content Creation Company)

English copy-editing:
Zeina Assaf;
Zoe Wildsmith
(The Content Creation Company)

Photoengraving:
Agence Point II

First edition, 2023
© Kaph Books, Beirut, 2023
© Department of Culture
and Tourism – Abu Dhabi, 2023
© France Muséums, Paris, 2023

ISBN: 978-614-8035-52-4
(English edition)

Printed in November 2022
by die Keure, Belgium
Legal deposit: January 2023

KAPH
ART BOOKS FROM THE MIDDLE EAST

Gouraud Street, Gemmayze
Renno Building, 3rd floor
Beirut, Lebanon
www.kaphbooks.com

Distribution:
Les Presses du Réel, France
www.lespressesdureel.com

Idea Books, The Netherlands
www.ideabooks.nl

ARTBOOK LLC, USA
D.A.P. |
Distributed Art Publishers, Inc.
www.artbook.com

CIEL book distribution,
Dubai, UAE
www.ciel.me

Cover illustrations

Front cover

Jaba Chitrakar. *The 2007 Tsunami*. Bengal, India, 2007 (Paris, Musée du Quai Branly – Jacques Chirac)

Sarasvati, The Goddess of Arts and Poetry. North India, c. 1980 (Paris, Musée du Quai Branly – Jacques Chirac)

Deepika Padukone and Shahid Kapoor in *Padmaavat* (2018), directed by Sanjay Leela Bhansali

The Demon King Ravana. Purulia, West Bengal, India, c. 1990 (Paris, Musée du Quai Branly – Jacques Chirac)

Princess Sita Under a Tree. Andhra Pradesh, India, first half of the 20th century (Paris, Musée du Quai Branly – Jacques Chirac)

Poster for the film *Hoor-e-Arab* (1955), directed by Prem Narayan Arora

Aishwarya Rai in *Jodhaa Akbar* (2008), directed by Ashutosh Gowariker

Poster for the film *Rain* (*Barsaat*, 1949), directed by Raj Kapoor

Prince in his zenana. North India, Mughal school, c. 1740 (Paris, Bibliothèque Nationale de France)

Back cover

Ravi Varma (1848–1906). *Go Dohana*. Undated (Bangalore, Collection of Sandeep & Gitanjali Maini Foundation)

Poster for *Humayun* (1945), directed by Mehboob Khan

Deepika Padukone and Shahid Kapoor in *Padmaavat* (2018), directed by Sanjay Leela Bhansali

Krishna as a child playing the flute in *Kaliya Mardan* (1919), directed by Dadasaheb Phalke

Princess Sita Under a Tree. Andhra Pradesh, India, first half of the 20th century (Paris, Musée du Quai Branly – Jacques Chirac)

M G Ramchandran and J Jayalalitha in *Protector* (1967), directed by P Neelakantan

Hrithik Roshan in *Jodhaa Akbar* (2008), directed by Ashutosh Gowariker

Princess Sita Under a Tree. Andhra Pradesh, India, first half of the 20th century (Paris, Musée du Quai Branly – Jacques Chirac)

Krishna Dancing with the Cowherd Girls. Nathadwara, Rajasthan, India, 19th century (Paris, Musée du Quai Branly – Jacques Chirac)

Front flap

Ravi Varma (1848–1906). *Go Dohana*. Undated (Bangalore, Collection of Sandeep & Gitanjali Maini Foundation)

Deepika Padukone and Shahid Kapoor in *Padmaavat* (2018), directed by Sanjay Leela Bhansali

Krishna as a child playing the flute in *Kaliya Mardan* (1919), directed by Dadasaheb Phalke

Princess Sita Under a Tree. Andhra Pradesh, India, first half of the 20th century (Paris, Musée du Quai Branly – Jacques Chirac)

Back flap

Poster for the film *Hoor-e-Arab* (1955), directed by Prem Narayan Arora

Poster for the film *Rain* (*Barsaat*, 1949), directed by Raj Kapoor

Hrithik Roshan in *Jodhaa Akbar* (2008), directed by Ashutosh Gowariker

The Demon King Ravana. Purulia, West Bengal, India, c. 1990 (Paris, Musée du Quai Branly – Jacques Chirac)

Prince in his zenana. North India, Mughal school, c. 1740 (Paris, Bibliothèque Nationale de France)